태권도 자유품새 교과서

TAEKWONDO FREESTYLE POOMSAE GUIDE BOOK

• 저자 l 김상명, 전민우, 임승민, 전재준, 오철희,
허재성, 지호철, 지호용, 김근호

상아기획

태권도 자유품새 교과서
TAEKWONDO FREESTYLE POOMSAE GUIDE BOOK

저 자 / 김상명, 전민우, 임승민, 전재준, 오철희, 허재성, 지호철, 지호용, 김근호
초판발행 / 2023년 7월 5일
발행인 / 문상필
디자인 / 이태진, 권태궁
발행사 / 상아기획
등록번호 / 제318-1997-000041호
주   소 / 서울시 영등포구 경인로82길 3-4, 715호 (문래동1가, 센터플러스)
대표전화 / 02-2164-2700
팩스번호 / 02-6499-8864
홈페이지 / www.tkdsanga.com
이 메 일 / 0221642700@daum.net

ISBN / 979-11-86196-28-1   13690
가격 / 25,000원

저작권은 개발자에게 있습니다. 저자와 협의로 인지를 생략합니다.
* 잘못 만들어진 책은 구매하신 서점에서 교환해드립니다.

Printed in KOREA

저자소개

김상명
- WTPTA 상무이사
- 2018 자카르타-팔렘방 아시안게임 이란 대표팀 코치
- 남창도장 수석사범

전민우
- WTPTA 대표
- 경희대학교 품새감독
- 전 대한민국대표팀 코치

임승민
- 캐나다 국가대표 감독
- 팬암 태권도 연맹 품새지도위원
- 전 우크라이나 국가대표팀 코치

전재준
- 트리플제이 대표
- 경희대학교 품새부 기술코치
- WTPTA 상무이사
- 대한태권도협회 강사

오철희
- 국가대표경희대안화태권도장 관장
- 경희대학교 겸임교수
- WTPTA 상무이사

허재성
- 화성의과학대학교 스포츠건강학부 태권도전공 교수
- WTPTA 상무이사

지호철
- 백석대학교 스포츠과학부 태권도전공 교수
- 2022 고양세계태권도선수권대회 +30 단체전 우승
- 2017 타이페이하계유니버시아드대회 단체전 우승
- Director WTPTA

지호용
- 국가대표 TS태권도장 대표
- 2022 고양세계태권도선수권대회 +30 단체전 우승
- 전 필리핀 국가대표팀 코치
- Director WTPTA

김근호
- 글로벌 태권도장 관장
- WTPTA 사무처장

Authors Profile

Kim, Sangmyung, Ph.D
- Director, WTPTA
- Former Iran National Team Coach
- Namchangdojang Head Master

Jeon, Minwoo, Ph.D
- President, WTPTA
- Korean National Team Coach
- Kyunghee University. Head Coach

Rim, Seoungmin, ChPC, ATC
- Head Coach, Canadian National Team
- Director, WTPTA
- Poomsae instructor, Pan American Taekwondo Union
- Former Ukraine National Team Coach

Jeon, Jaejun
- Master Instructor, TripleJ
- Technical Coach, Kyunghee University. Poomsae Team
- Director, WTPTA

Oh, Chulhee, Ph.D
- Adjunct Professor, Kyunghee University
- President, KHU Anhwa Taekwondo
- Director, WTPTA

Huh, Jaesung, Ph.D
- Assistant Professor, Hwasung Medi-Science University
- Director, WTPTA

Ji, Hochul, Ph.D
- Professor of Taekwondo, Department of Sports Science, Baekseok University
- 2022 Goyang World Poomsae Championships-Over 30 Team Gold medalist
- 2017 Taipei Universiades-Gold medalist
- Director WTPTA

Ji, Hoyong
- TS Taekwondo Master
- 2022 Goyang World Poomsae Championships-Over 30 Team Gold medalist
- Former Phillipines National Team Coach
- Director WTPTA

Kim, Geunho
- Master Instructor, Global Taekwondo
- Director WTPTA

서문

태권도 품새종목은 2018 자카르타-팔램방 아시안게임 이후 겨루기와 더불어 관중들과 매스컴으로부터 많은 관심을 받고 있습니다. 특히 자유품새는 화려한 발기술과 태권도의 다양한 기술을 음악과 함께 선보이며 겨루기 경기와는 다른 매력을 선사하고 있습니다. 오늘 태권도 품새경기에 대한 관심은 공인품새 뿐만 아니라 자유품새의 발전도 큰 몫을 담당하고 있습니다. 그러나 아직 선수층이 두텁지 않고 저변확대가 느리게 진행되고 있습니다. 그 이유는 기술의 난도가 높고 이에 따른 진입장벽이 공인품새 보다 높기 때문입니다. 이 책은 지도자와 자유품새 선수를 희망하는 꿈나무들을 위해 저술 되었습니다. 자유품새 분야에 대한 간략한 이해와 응용기술의 구성방법, 필수 기술에 대한 지도방법을 담았습니다. 글보다는 QR코드를 통해 영상을 제공하여 독자들이 이해를 쉽게 하도록 노력하였습니다. 자유품새 선수들의 기량은 빠른 속도로 발전하고 있습니다. 그러나 아직 기술의 명칭, 용어들은 정립되지 않았기에 저희 집필진의 관점에서 기술된 점을 양지하시기 바랍니다. 가장 기본적인 내용을 담았으며 각 기술들의 활용은 독자들의 몫으로 남겨두었습니다. 이 책이 출판될 수 있도록 도와주신 모든 분들게 감사드리며 아직 척박한 자유품새 경기에 조그마한 단비가 되기를 바랍니다.

2023년 저자 일동

Introduction

Poomsae earned its popularity after successfully debuting at the 2018 Jakarta-Palembang Asian Games and the 2019 Lima Pan American Games, where it drew the attention of both the public and media. In particular, freestyle Poomsae attracted people with its various advanced kicking techniques performed to music.

The popularity of freestyle Poomsae today can be attributed both to its own development as well as the efforts of recognized Poomsae.

However, Freestyle Poomsae has a steeper learning curve than recognized Poomsae due to its higher technical difficulty. This has limited the number of actively competing freestyle athletes.

This is the first ever freestyle Poomsae book of its kind for coaches, athletes, as well as Taekwondo practitioners aspiring to become freestyle Poomsae athletes.

This book contains information about understanding freestyle Poomsae, its fundamentals, the application of techniques, as well as composition methods. There are also QR codes in the book that are linked to videos that will help readers understand the content more easily.

That being said, the skills of freestyle athletes have been evolving quickly, and official terminologies have yet to be developed. So we ask for your understanding with regard to the terminologies used in this book, as they have been developed by the authors.

Although this book contains the fundamentals, it is up to the readers to apply what they have learned and further develop their own skills.

We would like to thank everyone who helped publish this book, and we hope that it will be a helpful tool and freestyle Poomsae resource.

Authors

목차 Contents

01

1. 자유품새 Freestyle Poomsae ··· 19

    1) 대한민국 태권도 The Republic of Korea's Taekwondo ················· 21

    2) 태권도 품새의 경기화
        Development of Poomsae as a Competitive Sport ·············· 22

    3) 국제경기의 시작
        Beginning Globalization of Poomsae Competition ············· 24

    4) 공인품새의 한계 The Limits of Recognized Poomsae ················ 25

    5) 새품새 시작 The Beginning of New Poomsae ······························ 27

    6) 자유품새 도입 Introduction of Freestyle Poomsae ······················ 28

    7) 태권도 품새경기 변천사
        History of Taekwondo Poomsae Competition ··················· 31

02

2. 태권도 기본기술 Taekwondo Basic Techniques ································· 29

    1) 손기술 Hand Techniques ·· 40
        ① 공격기술 - 지르기 Attacking Techniques – Punches ············ 41
        ② 공격기술 - 찌르기 Attacking Techniques – Thrusts ··············· 43
        ③ 공격기술 - 치기 Attacking Techniques – Strikes ····················· 45
        ④ 공격기술 - 찍기 Attacking Techniques – Poke ························ 47
        ⑤ 방어기술 - 막기 Defensive Techniques – Blocks ···················· 48

⑥ 방어기술 - 빼기
   Defensive Techniques - Pulling Out ·················51
⑦ 방어기술 - 피하기
   Defensive Techniques - Dodging ·················52

2) 손기술 구성방법 Hand Techniques Composition Method ·········54
   ① 쳐막기 형태의 방어+공격
      Defensive Counter Blocks + Attacks ·················55
   ② 걷어막기 형태의 방어+공격
      Deflecting Types of Defensive Techniques + Attacks ··········58
   ③ 속도 및 리듬의 변화에 따른 동작 구성
      Composition based on the Speed and Rhythm of the Techniques
      ···60

3) 발기술 Foot Techniques ·················62
   ① 공격기술 - 차기 Attacking Techniques - Kicks ·················63

4) 발기술 구성방법 Composition Methods with Foot Techniques ······ 67
   ① 거듭차기 Repeating Kick ·················68
   ② 섞어차기 Combination Kick ·················70
   ③ 속도 및 리듬에 따른 동작 구성 Composition of Movements based on
      the Speed and Rhythm ·················71

5) 서기 및 딛기 Stances and Foootworks ·················72
   ① 서기 Stances ·················73

6) 서기 및 딛기 구성방법
   Composition Method with Stances and Footworks ·················75
   ① 서기와 딛기의 연결구성 Connecting Stances and Footworks ······76

7) 특수동작 Special Techniques ……………………………………… 78

03

3. 자유품새의 응용 기술
Application techniques of Freestyle Poomsae ………… 81

1) 뛰어옆차기 Jumping Sidekick ………………………………… 83
　① 뛰어 옆차기 〈지면〉 Jumping Side Kick 〈Ground〉 ………… 84
　② 뛰어 옆차기 〈공중〉 Jumping Side Kick 〈Air〉 …………… 85
　③ 뛰어 옆차기 〈자세〉 Jumping Side Kick 〈Posture〉 ……… 86
　④ 뛰어 옆차기 〈도약〉 Jumping Side Kick 〈Jump〉 ………… 87
　⑤ 뛰어 옆차기 Jumping Side Kick ……………………………… 88

2) 뛰어 앞차기 Multiple Front Kicks in a Jump …………………… 89
　① 번갈아 앞차기 Switching Front Kick ……………………… 90
　② 도약발 앞차기 Front Kick with the Jumping leg …………91
　③ 연속 차기 Consecutive Kicks ………………………………… 92
　④ 뛰어 앞차기 〈정확성〉 Jumping Front Kick 〈Accuracy〉 …93
　⑤ 뛰어 앞차기 3~5단계 Jumping Front Kick Steps 3~5 …94

3) 회전 발차기 Gradient of Spins in a Spin Kick ………………… 95
　① 540° 뒤후려차기 〈회전축 연습〉
　　　540° Spining Hook Kick 〈Training a Stable Rotational Axis〉　96
　② 돌개차기 Tornado Kick ………………………………………… 97
　③ 540° 뒤후려차기 〈시선〉 540° Spinning Hook Kick 〈Gaze〉 ……… 98
　④ 540° 뒤후려차기 540° Spinning Hook Kick ………………… 99
　⑤ 720° 돌개차기 〈회전 자세〉
　　　720° Roundhouse Kick 〈Rotating Position〉……………… 100

⑥ 720° 돌개차기 〈회전각〉
　720° Roundhouse Kick 〈Gradient angle〉 ·················· 101
⑦ 720° 돌개차기 〈착지〉 720° Roundhouse Kick 〈Landing〉 ········ 102
⑧ 720° 돌개차기 720° Roundhouse Kick ················· 103

4) 연속발차기 Kyorugi Style Consecutive Kicking ·········· 104
　① 나래차기 Double Roundhouse Kick ················· 105
　② 상단 돌려차기 High Section Roundhouse Kick ········ 106
　③ 돌개차기 Kyorugi Style Tornado Kick ················ 107
　④ 연속발차기 〈구성 예시〉
　　Kyorugi Style Consecutive Kicks 〈Examples〉 ·········· 108

5) 아크로바틱 Acrobatics ···························· 109
　① 물구나무서기 Handstand ························ 110
　② 물구나무서기 〈이동〉 Handstand 〈Moving〉 ············ 111
　③ 물구나무서기 〈두발 착지〉 Handstand 〈Landing〉········ 112
　④ 측전 〈시작〉 Roundoff 〈Start〉 ···················· 113
　⑤ 측전 〈진행〉 Roundoff 〈progression〉 ··············· 114
　⑥ 측전 〈착지〉 Roundoff 〈Landing〉 ·················· 115

6) 뒤공중 Backflip ································· 116
　① 뒤공중 〈기초〉 Backflip 〈Basics〉 ···················117
　② 뒤공중 〈도약〉 Backflip 〈Jump〉 ····················118
　③ 뒤공중 〈말기〉 Backflip 〈Rolling〉 ·················· 119
　④ 뒤공중 〈착지〉 Backflip 〈Landing〉 ················· 120
　⑤ 뒤공중 Backflip ·····························121
　⑥ 측전 뒤공중 Roundoff Backflip ··················· 122
　⑦ 측전 이어차기 Roundoff Backflip with Multiple Kicks ········ 123

7) 모돌개차기 B-twist kick ··· 124
   ① 모돌기 Butterfly ··· 125
   ② 모돌개차기 〈비틀기〉 B-twist kick 〈Twisting〉 ··········· 126
   ③ 모돌개차기 〈모돌아 360°〉 B-twist kick 〈B-twist〉 ······ 127
   ④ 모아 돌개차기 Pop Tornado Kick ························· 128
   ⑤ 모돌개차기 B-twist kick ··································· 129

8) 휘돌개차기 Corkscrew kick ··· 130
   ① 휘돌개차기 〈회전〉 Corkscrew kick 〈Rotation〉 ··········· 131
   ② 휘돌개차기 〈동선〉 Corkscrew kick 〈Moving line〉 ······ 132
   ③ 휘돌개차기 〈휘돌기〉 Corkscrew kick 〈Cheat Gainer〉 ··· 133
   ④ 휘돌개차기 〈휘돌아 360°〉 Corkscrew kick 〈Corkscrew〉 · 134
   ⑤ 휘돌개차기 Corkscrew kick ······························· 135

9) 옆돌아 돌개차기 Cartwheel full twist kick ······················· 136
   ① 옆돌기 Cartwheel ··· 137
   ② 짚고 후려차기 후 모아 돌개차기
      Touch Hook Kick followed by a Pop Tornado Kick ······ 138
   ③ 옆돌아 돌개차기 Cartwheel full twist kick ················· 139

10) 짚기 Scoot - Touch Down Rise ··································· 140
   ① 안짚기 Scoot ·· 141
   ② 안짚기 - 휘돌기 〈연결〉 Scoot - Cheat Gainer 〈Connection〉 ······ 142
   ③ 안짚기 - 휘돌기 Scoot - Cheat Gainer ····················· 143
   ④ 바깥짚기 〈회전〉 Touch Down Rise 〈Spin〉 ··············· 144
   ⑤ 바깥짚기 〈동선〉 Touch Down Rise 〈Moving line〉 ······ 145
   ⑥ 바깥짚기 Touch Down Rise ································ 146

11) 기술 강화 훈련 Skill-Enhancement Training ··················· 147

① 점프 런지 스쿼트 Jump Lunge Squat ·············147
② 도약 후 다리 모으기
　　Gathering the Legs Together After Jumping ·············148
③ 보조기구 뛰어 넘기 Jumping Over Training Equipment ·············149
④ 제자리 도약 차기 Stationary Jump Kicking ·············150
⑤ 속도 차기 Speed Kicking ·············151
⑥ 공중 연속차기 Consecutive Kicks in Midair ·············152
⑦ 연속 발차기 〈딛기〉
　　Kyorugi Style Consecutive Kicking 〈Footwork〉 ·············153
⑧ 무릎 올리기 Knee Ups ·············155
⑨ 뒤공중 〈두발차기〉 Backflip 〈Straddle kick〉 ·············157
⑩ 뒤공중 〈이어차기〉 Backflip 〈Multiple Kick〉 ·············158
⑪ 뒤공중 〈뒤후려차기〉 Backflip 〈T-Grab Spinning Hook〉 ·············159

12) 기술 차기의 응용 Variation of Kicks ·············160
　　① 모돌아 바깥차기 B-twist Illusion Kick ·············160
　　② 뒤후려차기 - 모돌개차기 Hook Kick - B-twist Kick ·············161
　　③ 모돌아 360° - 휘돌개차기 B-twist - Corkscrew kick ·············162
　　④ 휘돌아 바깥차기 Corkscrew Illusion Kick ·············163
　　⑤ 안짚기 -〉 휘돌개차기 Scoot- Corkscrew Kick ·············164
　　⑥ 돌개차기 -〉 휘돌개차기 Tornado Kick - Corkscrew kick ·············165
　　⑦ 옆돌아 540° 후려차기 Hyper Hook Kick ·············166
　　⑧ 옆돌아 연속 후려차기 Shuriken Hyper Hook Kick ·············167
　　⑨ 옆돌아 720° Cartwheel Full Twist Double ·············168

기술용어 정리 Glossary ·············169
참고문헌 References ·············170
도움주신분들 ·············171

1

자유품새

1. Freestyle Poomsae

1 자유품새 FreeStyle Poomsae

1) 대한민국 태권도
The Republic of Korea's Taekwondo

2) 태권도 품새의 경기화
Development of Poomsae as a Competitive Sport

3) 국제경기의 시작
Beginning Globalization of Poomsae Competition

4) 공인품새의 한계
The Limits of Recognized Poomsae

5) 새품새 시작
The Beginning of New Poomsae

6) 자유품새 도입
Introduction of Freestyle Poomsae

7) 태권도 품새경기 변천사
History of Taekwondo Poomsae Competition

1.Freestyle Poomsae

1) 대한민국 태권도

태권도, 대한민국 국기(國技)이며 현재 전 세계 5개 대륙에 210개의 회원국을 보유하고 있다.

태권도 수련인구는 약 1억명 이상으로 대한민국을 대표하는 전통 무예의 상징이다. 국내는 물론 전 세계인들이 수련하고 많은 사랑을 받고 있으며, 태권도 수련 인구는 점차 확산되고 있는 추세이다.

태권도는 경기화를 통해 스포츠로 발전하였다. 가장 먼저 경기화된 겨루기는 2000년 시드니 올림픽 정식 종목으로 채택되면서 세계적인 스포츠로 자리매김하였으며 품새는 2018년 아시안게임과 팬암게임에 정식 종목으로 채택되면서 그 뒤를 이어가고 있다.

1) The Republic of Korea's Taekwondo

Taekwondo is a national sport of the Republic of Korea.

It is a Korean traditional martial art that is practiced and loved by both people living in Korea and across the entire world.
Currently, 210 nations in five different continents practice Taekwondo. Worldwide, there are about one hundred million practitioners, but this number is continuing to grow.

Taekwondo gained its reputation through its competitions. Kyorugi (sparring) was the first Taekwondo discipline to become a competitive sport. Taekwondo Kyorugi (sparring) became a global sport when it was adopted as an official event in the Sydney Olympics in the year 2000. In 2018, Poomsae was adopted into the Asian Games and in 2019, it was adopted into the Pan American Games as an official event and continues to be a global sport to this day.

2) 태권도 품새의 경기화

태권도 품새는 1992년, 겨루기 경기 일변도에서 벗어나 태권도의 무도성 회복과 다양성의 홍보, 그리고 침체된 성인 태권도와 태권도장의 활성화를 위하여 대한태권도협회에서 주관한 제1회 태권도 한마당대회가 개최되었다.

태권도 한마당은 품새, 격파, 호신술, 태권체조 등 태권도의 전반적인 종목에 걸쳐 다양한 연령대의 수련생들이 본인의 기량을 발휘하고 태권도의 우수성을 알릴 수 있도록 기획되었다.

대한태권도협회에서 주관하고 있던 태권도한마당은 1999년부터 국기원이 이어받아 현재까지 매년 개최하고 있으며, 2004년부터는 국제대회로 변모하여 세계 태권도인들의 축제로 불리며 명실상부한 태권도 경연대회로 자리 잡고 있다.

2) Development of Poomsae as a competitive sport.

In 1992, the Korean Taekwondo Association hosted the first Taekwondo Hanmadang Competition in order to restore Taekwondo's identity as a martial arts, display its multifaceted nature, renew its popularity in adults, and revitalize its dojangs. It was at this first Hanmadang that Taekwondo Poomsae first broke away from Kyorugi (sparring) and became a competitive sport in its own right.

The Taekwondo Hanmadang Competition gave Taekwondo practitioners the opportunity to demonstrate their skills and promote Taekwondo's excellence across all of its disciplines, including poomsae, breaking techniques, self-defense, and Taekwondo gymnastics.

The Taekwondo Hanmandang Competition was first hosted by the Korean Taekwondo Association, but it was handed off to the Kukkiwon in 1999 and has since been hosted annually by the organization. The Taekwondo Hanmandang became an international competition in 2004, and it is now considered a festival for Taekwondo practitioners across the globe. At present day, it has established its place as a true competition within the Taekwondo community.

1. Freestyle Poomsae

당시 태권도한마당에서 진행된 품새 경기는 경연에 가까웠으며, 유급자 품새와 단체전 품새로 구성되는 공인품새 경연 부문과 참가자들이 직접 품새를 창안하여 단체전으로 구성하는 창작 품새 경연 부문이 함께 진행되었다.

태권도한마당은 현재 품새 경기의 초석이 되었으며, 이후 1998년 제8회 용인대학교 총장기 전국남여고등학교 태권도 대회를 시작으로 각 대학 총장기(배)에서 품새대회가 신설 되었다.
또한 2004년 제1회 대한태권도협회장배 전국 태권도품새선수권 대회가 개최되었고, 2006년에는 대한태권도협회에서 공식적으로 품새경기규칙을 제정하여 경기대회의 요건을 갖추기 시작하였다.

경기규칙 제정이후 제1회 세계 태권도 품새선수권대회(2006년)가 개최되면서 품새의 저변확대와 세계화에 기여를 하였다.

At first, the Poomsae competitions held at the Taekwondo Hanmadang were not yet official competitions. The competitions consisted of individual and team divisions, where competitors performed recognized Poomsae, or creative Poomsae that was made by each of the competing teams.

The Taekwondo Hanmandang was the beginning of Poomsae competitions as we know them today. Following in the footsteps of the Hanmandang, Yongin University President's 8th National Boys and Girls' High School Taekwondo Competition featured Poomsae for the first time in 1998. Other universities quickly followed suit.

In 2004, the 1st National Taekwondo Poomsae Championships were held by the Korean Taekwondo Association. This was quickly followed by the development of formal Poomsae competition rules and regulations in 2006 After the establishment of these competitive rules and regulations, the 1st World Taekwondo Poomsae Championships were held in 2006, contributing to the expansion and globalization of Taekwondo Poomsae.

1. 자유품새

3) 국제경기의 시작

2000년 4월 17일 프랑스 파리에서 열린 세계태권도연맹 상임이사회에서 품새 대회를 개최하기로 결정하였고, 그 결과 2006년 9월 4일부터 6일까지 서울 올림픽공원 제2체육관(체조경기장)에서 제1회 세계 태권도 품새 선수권 대회가 개최되었다.

59개국 590여명의 선수단이 참가한 제1회 세계 태권도 품새 선수권 대회는 국제경기로써 태권도 품새의 세계화를 알린 대회로 그 의미가 크다.

이후 2009년 세르비아 베오그라드에서 개최된 하계유니버시아드대회에 정식종목으로 채택되었고 2010년 제11회 세계 대학 태권도 선수권 대회, 2018년 자카르타-팔렘방 아시안게임과 2019년 리마 판암 게임의 정식종목으로 채택되면서 올림픽 정식 종목인 겨루기와 함께 세계인의 스포츠로 크게 성장하고 있다.

3) Beginning globalization of Poomsae competition

On April 17th, 2000, in Paris, France, the executive board of directors of the World Taekwondo Federation made the decision to designate Poomsae as an official Taekwondo competition discipline. Consequently, the 1st World Taekwondo Poomsae Championships were held at Seoul Olympic Park from September 4th-6th, 2006.

590 athletes from 59 countries participated in the 1st World Taekwondo Poomsae Championships. This international competition marked the start of the globalization of Taekwondo Poomsae.

At the 2009 Summer Universiade hosted in Belgrade, Serbia, Taekwondo Poomsae was chosen as an official event. Poomsae also became an official event at both the 11th World University Taekwondo Championships in 2010, the Jakarta-Palembang Asian Games in 2018, and the Lima Pan American Games in 2019. The popularity of Taekwondo's Poomsae discipline continues to grow rapidly alongside the Olympic sport of Kyorugui around the world.

4) 공인품새의 한계

품새의 경기화를 시작으로 많은 태권도 지도자들이 품새에 대한 관심이 크게 증가하였고 전문적인 선수들을 양성하는 계기가 되었다. 하지만 1960~70년대에 제작된 유급자품새와 유단자품새는 태권도 수련 및 보급을 목적으로 제작되어 많은 한계점이 나타나고 있다.

이에 품새 경기의 빠른 활성화에 따른 경기력의 상향 평준화와 기존 공인품새 기술의 단조로움 등 여러 한계점을 개선하고자 새품새 및 자유품새를 도입하여 대회를 개최하는 등 여러 시도가 나타나기 시작하였다.

향후 국제 스포츠종목으로 발전되는 과정에서 품새경기의 기틀을 확고히 하고 지속적인 발전을 할 수 있도록 다양한 관점에서 접근이 필요한 상황이다.

심판 판정의 객관성과 공정성 그리고 신뢰성의 중요함에 중점이 실리면서 감점의 채점방식 도입, 심판의 오심 정도에 대한 등급제 등 현재의 채점 방식과 공정성에 대한 변화의 촉구를 바라는 학계와 현장 지도자의 목소리가 점점 증가하였다.

현재 품새 대회 경기는 개인·복식·단체전으로 구분하여 다양한 종목으로 시행되고 있으며, 경기방식은 일리미네이션 토너먼트 방식, 컷오프(단계별 점수제) 방식, 혼합방식(컷오프 방식 + 토너먼트 방식) 등으로 진행되고 있다. 공인품새 경기는 부별로 지정된 품새 가운데 지정 또는 추첨하여 정할 수 있다.

4) The Limits of Recognized Poomsae

As Poomsae continued becoming known as a sport in its own right, many Taekwondo instructors became increasingly interested in it. Interested individuals started training athletes to specialize competitively in Poomsae. However, there were many limitations in the Poomsae created between the 1960's-1970's because the purpose of Poomsae was for training general practitioners, and for the dissemination of Taekwondo.

The repetitive nature of Recognized Poomsae, the rapidly advancing technical skills of competitors, and the desire to address other problematic aspects of Poomsae competitions resulted in numerous attempts to introduce new styles of Poomsae competition, such as Freestyle Poomsae.
In order to continue to develop and solidify Poomsae's claim to the world's sporting stage, an approach that took a variety of different perspectives into consideration was required.

The voices of Taekwondo coaches and academics called for a more fair and objective system for scoring Poomsae. They wanted a system that would include things such as a scoring system for deductions, and a system for detecting the degree of personal bias in each judge.

Currently, there are a wide variety of different types of Poomsae competitions that are divided into individual, pair, and team categories. Competitions are held using single elimination, a cut-off system, or a combination of these two competition styles (cut-off + single elimination). The specific poomsae required for each division in Recognized Poomsae competitions are either chosen by the officials or determined by a random draw. Competition poomsae is divided into colour-belt poomsae (Taegeuk 3 – Taegeuk 8) and blackbelt Poomsae (Koryo – Hansu). Furthermore, World Taekwondo has added Freestyle Poomsae competitions to be held alongside Recognized Poomsae competitions.

5) 새품새 시작

아시아태권도연맹은 2016년 품새 세계화 사업을 위해 문화체육관광부로부터 지원을 받아 10여종의 새품새를 개발하였으며, 새롭게 개발된 새품새는 연령에 따라 구분되었다.

18세 미만의 경우 힘차리와 야망, 18세 이상 30세 이하의 경우 새별, 나르샤, 비각, 30세 이상 50세 이하의 경우 어울림, 새아라, 50세 이상 60세 이하의 경우 한솔, 나래, 온누리 품새가 제작되었다.

이 중 비각, 힘차리, 나르샤, 새별의 경기용 품새는 2018년 호치민에서 열린 제5회 아시아 태권도 품새 선수권 대회, 2018년 제18회 자카르타-팔렘방 아시안게임 태권도 품새 경기 종목에서 공인품새, 자유품새와 함께 도입되었다.

5) The Beginning of New Poomsae

In 2016, after receiving funding from the Ministry of Culture, Sports and Tourism for a Poomsae globalization project, the Asian Taekwondo Federation developed 10 new Poomsae, which were classified based on age.

For 18 and under, Heem-cha-rhee and Yah-mang; for 18 to 30, Sae-byeol, Na-reu-sha, and Bi-gak; from 30 to under 50, Uh-ool-eem and Sae-ara; and for 50 to 60, Han-sol, Na-rae, and Ohn-nuri Poomsae were made.

Bi-gak, Heem-cha-rhee, Na-reu-sha and Sae-byeol were introduced as competition Poomsae at the 5th Asian Taekwondo Poomsae Championships held in Ho Chi Minh in 2018, and the 18th Jakarta-Palembang Asian games in 2018, and were performed alongside Recognized and Freestyle Poomsae.

6) 자유품새 도입

공인품새의 기술적 한계성과 경기로서의 문제점들을 보완하기 위하여 다양한 기술동작과 연속 차기 등 태권도의 전체적인 요소와 아크로바틱을 활용한 태권도기술이 혼합된 자유품새가 도입되었다.

자유품새는 기존의 공인품새와는 달리 겨루기의 딛기와 연속 차기, 시범의 도약 차기, 회전 발차기, 아크로바틱을 이용하여 시연자가 자유롭게 구성하는 품새 경기이다. 또한 태권도 기술을 바탕으로 음악과 안무가 함께 어우러진 품새를 말하며, 이는 태권도의 모든 동작들을 이해하여 자기 자신이 생각하고 있는 동작의 이미지를 객관적인 형식으로 나타내는 종목이다.
자유품새는 2011년 블라디보스톡에서 개최된 제6회 세계 태권도 품새 선수권 대회에서 시범종목으로 채택되었고, 2012년 콜롬비아 제7회 세계 태권도 품새 선수권대회에 정식종목으로 채택되었다.

2017년 대만 타이베이 하계유니버시아드대회에서 자유품새 경기규칙이 적용되어 처음으로 한국선수들이 자유품새를 포함한 태권도 품새경기에 참여할 수 있었다.
2018년 베트남 호치민에서 개최된 제5회 아시아태권도선수권대회에서 자유품새를 경기종목으로 도입하면서 빠르게 발전하는 계기를 마련하였다. 같은 해의 제18회 자카르타-팔렘방 아시안게임에서 자유품새가 도입되면서 자유품새에 대한 관심이 국내외적으로 크게 높아지게 되었다.

| 2017 타이페이 하계 유니버시아드대회 자유품새 한국 첫 출전 | 2018년 대만 세계 품새선수권대회 자유품새부문 한국 첫 출전 |

6) Introduction of Freestyle Poomsae

To compensate for the technical limitations of Recognized Poomsae and the competition-related problems associated with it, Freestyle Poomsae was introduced. Freestyle Poomsae is a style of Poomsae competition that incorporates the combined use of a wide variety of technical Taekwondo skills, including consecutive kicking, various technical movements and acrobatics.

Unlike the Recognized Poomsae style of competition, in Freestyle Poomsae, the athlete incorporates Kyorugi footworks, consecutive kicks, spinning kicks and acrobatics into their Poomsae and freely composes it. Using Taekwondo techniques as a backdrop, Freestyle Poomsae is choreographed to coexist harmoniously with a musical soundtrack.

The purpose this Poomsae competition style is to objectively convey one's own perception and imagery of all the different Taekwondo skills and techniques used in one's Freestyle Poomsae, so in order to choreograph Freestyle Poomsae, one must first understand the existing Taekwondo skills and techniques.

| First Korean to compete at the Summer Universiade Poomsae Competition held in Taiwan in 2017 | First Korean to compete at the World Poomsae Championships held in Taiwan in 2018 |

1. 자유품새

자유품새의 세부적인 기술로는 뛰어 옆차기, 뛰어 앞차기, 회전 발차기, 연속 차기, 아크로바틱으로 구분되어 있다. 자유품새에 관련하여 배점기준은 <표 1>과 같다.

The mandatory techniques of Freestyle Poomsae are comprised of the following: jumping side kick, multiple kicks in a jump, gradient of spins in a spin kick, Kyorugi style consecutive kicks, and acrobatic kicking technique. The scoring criteria for Freestyle Poomsae is shown below in <Table 1>

표 1. 자유 품새 배점표 (Table 1. Allotted Scoring Chart for Free Style Poomsae)

채점 항목 Scoring Criteria	세부 기준 항목 Details of Scoring Criteria		점수 Point
기술력 (6.0) Technical Skills (6.0)	차기 난이도 (5.0) Level of difficulty of foot techniques (5.0)	뛰어 옆차기 (뛴 높이) Jumping side kick	1.0
		뛰어 앞차기 (차기 수) Multiple kicks in a jump	1.0
		회전 발차기 (회전각) Gradient of spins in a spin kick	1.0
		겨루기방식 연속 차기 Kyorugi style consecutive kicks	1.0
		아크로바틱 차기 동작 Acrobatic kicking technique	1.0
	기본 동작 및 실용성 Basic movements & Practicability		1.0
연출성 (4.0) Presentation (4.0)	창의성 Creativeness		4.0
	조화 Harmony		
	기의포현 Expression of energy		
	음악 및 안무 Music & choreography		
최대 점수 (10.0) Maximum Points			10.0

7) 태권도 품새경기 변천사
History of Taekwondo Poomsae Competition

대회명 Competition Name	연도 Year	경기 종목 Competition Type	주최 Host
제1회 세계태권도한마당 First Taekwondo Hanmadang Competition	1992	품새, 격파, 태권체조, 창작품새 Poomsae, Board Breaking, Taekwondo Aerobics, Freestyle Poomsae	대한태권도협회 (1999년 이후 국기원 주최) Korean Taekwondo Association (Organized by the Kukkiwon post 1991)
제8회 용인대학교 총장기 전국 남·녀 고등학교 태권도대회 8th Yongin University National High School Taekwondo Competition	1998	공인품새 개인전 Individual Recognized Poomsae	용인대학교 Yongin University
98 세계태권도문화축제 1998 World Taekwondo Cultural Festival	1998	공인품새 Recognized Poomsae	충청대학 Choongcheong University
제1회 춘천 코리아오픈국제태권도대회 First Chooncheon Taekwondo Korean International Open	2000	창작 품새 단체전 Creative Team Poomsae	대한태권도협회 Korean Taekwondo Association
제12회 경희대학교 총장기 전국 남·녀 고등학교 태권도대회 12th Kyunghee University National High School Taekwondo Competition	2000	공인품새 개인전, 단체전 Individual and Team Recognized Poomsae	경희대학교 Kyunghee University
제2회 코리아경주국제 여자 태권도 오픈대회 Second Korea Kyungjoo National Women's Taekwondo Open	2003	공인품새, 창작품새, 태권체조 Recognized Poomsae, Creative Poomsae, Taekwondo Aerobics	세계태권도연맹 World Taekwondo Federation
제1회 한국여성태권도연맹 회장배 전국여성태권도대회 First Korea Women Taekwondo Federation's President's Cup National Women's Taekwondo Competition	2003	공인품새 Recognized Poomsae	한국여성태권도연맹 Korea Women's Taekwondo Federation
제1회 우석대학교 총장기 전국품새대회 First Woosuk University President's National Poomsae Competition	2003	공인품새 개인전, 단체전, 창작 품새 단체전 Recognized Poomsae, Individual and Team Creative Poomsae Team Competition	우석대학교 Woosuk University
제1회 계명대학교 총장기 전국태권도품새대회 First Keimyung University President's National Taekwondo Poomsae Competition	2004	공인품새 개인전, 단체전 Individual and Team Recognized Poomsae	계명대학교 Keimyung University
제16회 아시아태권도선수권대회 16th Asian Taekwondo Championships	2004	공인품새 개인전, 단체전 Individual and Team Recognized Poomsae	아시아태권도연맹 Asian Taekwondo Federation
제5회 세계주니어태권도선수권대회 5th World Junior Taekwondo Championships	2004	공인품새 개인전, 단체전 Individual and Team Recognized Poomsae	세계태권도연맹 World Taekwondo Federation
제1회 대한태권도협회장배 전국태권도품새선수권대회 1st KTA Taekwondo Poomsae Championships	2004	공인품새 개인전, 단체전 Individual and Team Recognized Poomsae	대한태권도협회 Korean Taekwondo Association

1. 자유품새

태권도 품새경기 변천사
History of Taekwondo Poomsae Competition

대 회 명 Competition Name	연 도 Year	경기 종목 Competition Type	주최 Host
제1회 한국 중·고등학교 태권도연맹 회장배 품새대회 First Korea Junior Taekwondo Federation President's Cup Poomsae Competition	2005	공인품새 개인전, 복식전, 단체전 Individual, Pair and Team Recognized Poomsae	한국중고등학교태권도연맹 Korea Junior Taekwondo Federation
제1회 한국체육대학교 총장배 전국품새대회 First Korea Sports University President's Cup National Poomsae Competition	2005	공인품새 개인전, 복식전, 단체전 Individual, Pair and Team Recognized Poomsae	한국체육대학교 Korea Sports University
프레세계품새선수권대회 Pre World Poomsae Championships	2005	공인품새 개인전, 복식전, 단체전 Individual, Pair and Team Recognized Poomsae	대한태권도협회 Korea Taekwondo Association
제1회 동아대학교 총장배 전국 태권도 품새 대회 First Dong A University President's Cup National Taekwondo Poomsae Competition	2006	공인품새 개인전, 복식전, 단체전 Individual, Pair and Team Recognized Poomsae	동아대학교 Dong A University
제1회 세계태권도 품새선수권대회 First World Taekwondo Poomsae Championships	2006	공인품새 개인전, 복식전, 단체전 Individual, Pair and Team Recognized Poomsae	세계태권도연맹 World Taekwondo Federation
제1회 한국나사렛대학교 총장배 전국태권도품새대회 First Korea Nazareth University President's Cup National Taekwondo Poomsae Competition	2007	공인품새 개인전, 복식전, 단체전 Individual, Pair and Team Recognized Poomsae	한국나사렛대학교 Korea Nazareth University
제3회 한국실업태권도연맹 회장기 전국태권도대회 Third Korea Industrial Taekwondo Federation President's National Taekwondo Competition	2009	공인품새 개인전, 복식전, 단체전 Individual, Pair and Team Recognized Poomsae	한국실업태권도연맹 Korea Industrial Taekwondo Federation
제25회 하계유니버시아드대회 25th Summer Universiade Competition	2009	공인품새 개인전, 복식전, 단체전 Individual, Pair and Team Recognized Poomsae	국제대학스포츠연맹 International University Sports Federation
제1회 상지대학교 총장배 전국태권도품새대회 First Sangji University President' Cup National Taekwondo Poomsae Competition	2010	공인품새 개인전, 복식전, 단체전 Individual, Pair and Team Recognized Poomsae	상지대학교 Sangji University
제6회 세계품새선수권대회 6th World Poomsae Championships	2011	자유품새 시범종목 Freestyle Poomsae (Demonstration event)	세계태권도연맹 World Taekwondo Federation
제7회 세계품새선수권대회 7th World Poomsae Championships	2012	자유품새 정식종목 Freestyle Poomsae (Official event)	세계태권도연맹 World Taekwondo Federation
2014 전국종별태권도선수권대회 2014 National all divisions Taekwondo Championships	2014	공인품새 개인전, 복식전, 단체전 Individual, Pair and Team Recognized Poomsae	대한태권도협회 Korea Taekwondo Association

1.Freestyle Poomsae

태권도 품새경기 변천사
History of Taekwondo Poomsae Competition

대회명 Competition Name	연도 Year	경기 종목 Competition Type	주최 Host
제49회 대통령기 전국단체대항 태권도대회 49th National Team Taekwondo Competition for the Presidential Flag	2014	공인품새 개인전, 페어전, 단체전 Individual, Pair and Team Recognized Poomsae	대한태권도협회 Korean Taekwondo Association
제12회 한국체육대학교 총장배 전국품새대회 12th Korea Sports University National Poomsae Competition President's Cup	2016	자유품새 시범종목 Freestyle Poomsae (Demonstration event)	한국체육대학교 Korean National Sports Univiersity
제29회 하계유니버시아드대회 29th Summer Universiade	2017	공인품새(60%)+ 자유품새(40%) 개인전, 복식전, 단체전 Recognized (60%) + Freestyle Poomsae (40%) Individual, Pair, and Team	국제대학스포츠연맹 International University Sports Federation
제1회 WT비치태권도 1st WT Beach Taekwondo	2017	공인품새 개인전, 복식전, 단체전 자유품새 개인전, 복식전, 단체전 Individual, Pair and Team Recognized and Freestyle Poomsae	세계태권도연맹 World Taekwondo Federation
2017 춘천코리아오픈태권도대회 2017 Chuncheon Korea Open Taekwondo Competition	2017	공인품새 개인전, 복식전, 단체전 자유품새 개인전, 복식전, 단체전 새품새 개인전 시범종목 Individual, Pair and Team Recognized and Freestyle Poomsae New Poomsae Individual (Demonstration event)	대한태권도협회 Korea Taekwondo Association
제14회 대한태권도협회장배 전국태권도품새선수권대회 14th Korea Taekwondo Association President's Cup National Taekwondo Poomsae Championships	2017	공인품새 개인전, 복식전, 단체전 자유품새 개인전 Individual, Pair and Team Recognized Poomsae Individual Freestyle Poomsae	대한태권도협회 Korea Taekwondo Association
제52회 대통령기 전국 단체대항 태권도대회 52nd National President's Cup Team Competition	2017	공인품새 개인전, 페어전, 단체전 자유품새 개인전, 복식전, 단체전 Individual, Pair and Team Recognized and Freestyle Poomsae	대한태권도협회 Korea Taekwondo Association
제15회 한국여성태권도연맹 회장배 전국태권도대회 15th Korea Women's Taekwondo Federation's National Taekwondo President's Cup Competition	2017	공인품새 개인전, 페어전, 단체전 자유품새 개인전 Individual, Pair and Team Recognized Poomsae Individual Freestyle Poomsae	한국여성태권도연맹 Korea Women's Taekwondo Federation
제5회 아시아태권도품새 선수권대회 5th Asian Taekwondo Poomsae Championships	2018	공인품새 개인전, 복식전, 단체전 자유품새 개인전, 복식전, 단체전 새품새 Individual, Pair and Team Recognized and Freestyle Poomsae New Poomsae	아시아태권도연맹 Asian Taekwondo Federation
제18회 자카르타-팔렘방 아시안게임 18th Jakarta-Palembang Asian Games	2018	개인전 - 공인품새 + 새품새 단체전 - 공인품새 + 새품새 + 자유품새 Individual – Recognized + New Poomsae Team – Recognized + New + Freestyle Poomsae	아시아태권도연맹 Asian Taekwondo Federation

1. 자유품새

태권도 품새경기 변천사
History of Taekwondo Poomsae Competition

대회명 Competition Name	연도 Year	경기 종목 Competition Type	주최 Host
제30회 용인대학교 총장기 전국 남·녀 고등학교 태권도 대회 30th Yongin University President's Cup National High School Taekwondo Competition	2018	자유품새 도입 Introduction of Freestyle Poomsae	용인대학교 Yongin University
제31회 경희대학교 총장기 전국 남·녀 고등학교 태권도 대회 31st Kyunghee University President's Cup National High School Taekwondo Competition	2019	자유품새 도입 Introduction of Freestyle Poomsae	경희대학교 Kyunghee University

2

태권도 기본기술

2. Taekwondo Basic Techniques

2 태권도 기본 기술 Taekwondo Basic Techniques

1) 손기술
Hand Techniques

2) 손기술 구성방법
Hand Techniques Composition Method

3) 발기술
Foot Techniques

4) 발기술 구성방법
Composition Methods with Foot Techniques

5) 서기 및 딛기
Stances and Footworks

6) 서기 및 딛기 구성방법
Composition Method with Stances and Footworks

7) 특수동작
Special Techniques

2. Taekwondo Basic Techniques

자유품새는 태권도 동작을 응용하여 다양한 방법으로 구성할 수 있다.

본 장에서는 손기술과 발기술, 서기와 딛기, 특수동작으로 구분하여 각 동작들을 어떻게 응용할 수 있는지 제시하고자 한다.

태권도의 기본기술을 복합동작과 응용동작으로 구현할 수 있고, 그 외 기술의 강약과 완급을 통해 자유품새를 구성 할 수 있다.

Taekwondo movements can be used in a wide variety of ways to create Freestyle Poomsae.

This chapter is divided into hand and foot techniques, stances and footworks, as well as special techniques, and it will explain how to use each of these types of techniques.

Basic Taekwondo techniques can be combinations or applied movements, and Freestyle Poomsae can be created by varying the speed and power of these techniques.

1) 손기술

손기술은 공격과 방어동작 그리고 호흡을 조절하거나 몸의 기운을 조절하는 동작 등으로 구분된다.

본 장에서는 공격과 방어동작의 연결방법에 대해 설명하고자 한다.

기존 공인품새는 공격과 방어 동작이 주로 단일동작 및 최대 2~3개의 동작으로 구성되어있다. 한 서기자세에서 공격 또는 방어 동작이 각기 하나씩 실행되거나 많게는 2~3가지 동작이 실행된다. 하지만 자유품새는 공인품새의 형태에서 벗어나 연결의 형태와 리듬, 속도에 변화를 주면서 더욱 다양하게 표현할 수 있다.

태권도에서 공격 동작은 지르기, 찌르기, 치기 등이 있으며, 방어동작은 움직이는 형태에 따라 안막기, 바깥막기, 내려막기, 올려막기, 거들어 막기, 가위막기, 외산틀막기, 헤쳐막기 등이 있다. 또한 막는 형태에 따라 흘려막기와 쳐막기, 걷어막기 등이 있다. 각 동작은 목표부위에 따라 최하단에서 최상단까지 공격하거나 방어하게 되는 특징을 토대로 복합동작, 응용동작, 연결동작으로 구성할 수 있다.

1) Hand Techniques

Hand techniques are divided into offensive and defensive movements, as well as movements that either control breathing or body energy/state.

This chapter will explain ways to connect offensive and defensive movements.

In Recognized Poomsae, offensive and defensive techniques are mainly comprised of single movements or small combinations of 2-3 movements at most. In each stance, single offensive or defensive techniques are executed, with 2-3 techniques executed at most. However, the framework for Freestyle Poomsae differs largely from that of Recognized Poomsae, allowing for the freedom to incorporate a wide diversity of connecting movements, rhythms and speeds that allow for great freedom in expression.

In Taekwondo, offensive techniques include punches, thrusts, strikes, etc. Depending on the direction of the movement, defensive techniques include inward block, outward block, downward block, upward block, supporting block, scissors block, single mountain block, scatter block, etc.

Depending on the target area of each movement, offensive and defensive motions can range from the lowest to highest areas of the body. Furthermore, they can include complex motions, applied motions, or connecting motions.

2.Taekwondo Basic Techniques

(1) 공격기술 – 지르기

주먹으로 상대를 공격하는 기술이다.

주먹, 편주먹, 집게주먹 등으로 상대방의 급소를 공격하는 기술로서 지르기, 젖혀지르기, 돌려지르기, 뒤지르기 등으로 활용된다.

(1) Attacking Techniques – Punches

The following techniques are all attacks involving the use of fists.

Fists, half-clenched fists, pincers fists, etc., are all used to attack the opponent's vital points with punches, turn-over punches, turning punches, backward punches, etc.

[금강옆지르기]

[Geumkang Side Punch]

[ㄷ지르기]

[U-shape Punch]

[돌려지르기]

[Turning Side Punch]

[뒤지르기]

[Backward Punch]

[세워지르기]

[Upright Punch]

[아래지르기]

[Low Punch]

2. 태권도 기본기술

[옆지르기]

[Side Punch]

[젖혀지르기]

[Turn-over Punch]

[쳇다리지르기]

[Fork Punch]

[치지르기]

[Upper-Cut Punch]

[표적지르기]

[Target Punch]

2.Taekwondo Basic Techniques

(2) 공격기술 – 찌르기

손끝으로 상대를 공격하는 기술이다.

지르기 기술과 팔의 움직임은 같지만 사용 부위를 손끝과 같은 면적이 좁은 부위를 활용하여 상대방의 급소에 강한 충격을 전달할 수 있는 기술이다.

(2) Attacking Techniques – Thrusts

The following techniques use fingertips to attack an opponent.

Although the arm movements are identical to those used for punches, using fingertips allows for a stronger attack to the opponent's vital points because the smaller striking area increases the pressure delivered upon impact.

[편손끝 세워찌르기]

[Spear Hand Upright Thrust]

[편손끝 엎어찌르기]

[Spear Hand Palm Down Thrust]

[편손끝 젖혀찌르기]

[Spear Hand Turn-over Thrust]

2.Taekwondo Basic Techniques

(3) 공격기술 – 치기

바른 주먹과 손끝을 제외한 손의 부위를 사용하여 상대를 공격하는 기술이다.

팔꿈치을 굽혔다가 펴거나 굽힌 채로 몸의 회전력을 이용하여 목표물을 가격하는 기술로서 '지르기, 찌르기, 찍기'를 제외한 손으로 하는 모든 공격 기술이다.

(3) Attacking Techniques – Strikes

The following are hand techniques that do not use knuckles or fingertips to attack an opponent.

These hand techniques do not include punches, strikes and chops. Instead, they use a rotational force while the elbow is bent, or the force of extended/retracting the arm to hit the target or opponent.

[거들어 등주먹 앞치기]

[Supported Back Fist Forward Strike]

[당겨 등주먹 앞치기]

[Pulling Back Fist Forward Strike]

[당겨 턱치기]

[Pulling Jaw Strike]

[등주먹 바깥치기]

[Back Fist Outward Strike]

[등주먹 앞치기]

[Back Fist Forward Strike]

[메주먹 바깥치기]

[Hammer Fist Outward Strike]

2. 태권도 기본기술

[손날 내려치기]

[Knife Hand Downward Strike]

[손날등 안치기]

[Reverse Knife Hand Inward Strike]

[손날 비틀어치기]

[Knife Hand Twisting Strike]

[제비품 목치기]

[Swallow Shaped Neck Inward Strike]

[팔굽 돌려치기]

[Turning Elbow Strike]

[팔굽 뒤치기]

[Backward Elbow Strike]

[팔굽 올려치기]

[Upward Elbow Strike]

[팔굽 표적치기]

[Target Elbow Strike]

2.Taekwondo Basic Techniques

(4) 공격기술 – 찍기

모둠손끝으로 상대를 공격하는 기술이다.

다섯 손가락 또는 두 손가락 등 손가락의 첫 마디를 모아 손끝으로 휘둘러 치는 기술로 '내려찍기, 안찍기, 앞찍기' 등이 있다.

(4) Attacking Techniques – Poke

These techniques attack an opponent using fingertips gathered together.

Whether five fingers are used or two fingers are used, the fingertips are gathered, then swung in attacks such as 'downward poke', 'inside poke', 'forward poke', etc.

[모둠손끝 찍기]

[Combined Fingertips Poke]

2. 태권도 기본기술

(5) 방어기술 – 막기

손이나 팔, 발이나 다리 등을 이용하여 상대방의 공격으로부터 자신의 주요 신체 부위를 방어하는 기술이다.

상대방의 공격에 맞서거나 쳐내는 '쳐막기'

충격을 흡수하는 '받아막기'

공격을 미리 차단하는 '걸어막기'

밀어 내어 공격의 진행 방향을 바꾸는 '걸어막기' 등이 있다.

(5) Defensive Techniques - Blocks

Using the hand, arm, foot, or leg, these techniques defend one's main body parts from an opponent's attacks.

'Counter blocks' counter or strike the opponent's attacks.

'Damper blocks' absorb the impact of an opponent's attacks.

'Tripping blocks' anticipate attacks and block them pre-emptively.

'Deflecting blocks' change the direction of attacks by pushing them to the side.

[가위막기]

[Scissors Block]

[거들어 바깥막기]

[Supported Outward Block]

[금강 아래막기]

[Geumgang Low Block]

2. Taekwondo Basic Techniques

[몸통 안막기]

[Trunk Inward Block]

[손날등 바깥막기]

[Reverse Knife Hand Outward Block]

[손날 비틀어막기]

[Twisted Knife Hand Block]

[손날 쳐막기]

[Counter Knife Hand Block]

[손등 올려막기]

[Upward Knife Hand Block]

[안팔목 바깥막기]

[Outward Inside Wrist Block]

[안팔목 헤쳐막기]

[Inside Wrist Scatter Block]

[엇걸어 아래막기]

[Crossed Low Block]

[옆차막기]

[Side Kicking Block]

2. 태권도 기본기술

[올려막기]

[Upward Block]

[외산틀막기]

[Single Mountain Block]

[한손날 내려막기]

[Single Knife Hand Downward Block]

[헤쳐 산틀막기]

[Scatter Mountain Block]

[황소막기]

[Bull Horn Block]

[흘려막기]

[Deflecting Block]

2.Taekwondo Basic Techniques

(6) 방어기술 – 빼기

상대방에게 자신의 팔목이나 발목 등을 잡혔을 때에 관절을 틀거나 돌려 빼낼 수 있도록 하는 기술이다.

(6) Defensive Techniques – Pulling Out

These are techniques in which the individual twists or rotates their joints in order to pull away from an opponent who is holding onto a body part such as the wrist or ankle.

[밑으로 빼기]

[앞으로 빼기]

[Downward Pull Out]

[Forward Pull Out]

(7) 방어기술 – 피하기

상대방의 공격에 맞지 않도록 몸을 왼쪽이나 오른쪽으로 틀거나, 앞으로 숙이거나 뒤로 젖히며 상대방의 공격으로부터 피하는 기술이다.

(7) Defensive Techniques – Dodging

These are techniques where the opponent's attacks are avoided by turning aside to the left or right, or leaning forwards or backwards.

[숙여피하기]

[Ducking]

[젖혀피하기]

[Back Leaning]

2.Taekwondo Basic Techniques

[틀어피하기]

[Rolling]

2) 손기술 구성방법

한 품에 이루어지는 동작을 구성하는 방법은 태권도 동작을 이용하여 가상의 적을 상대로 방어하고 공격하는 다양한 기술체계를 구성하는 것이다.

이때 고려할 사항은 목표 부위이고, 중단 공격이라고 가정한다면 시연자는 중단 방어로 시작하여 공방을 이어 가게 되고 상단 공격을 가정한다면 상단 방어로 시작하는 것이다.

이처럼 상대의 최하단부터 최상단까지 선택적으로 목표를 삼아 공격동작 및 방어동작을 구성한다. 또한 막기의 형태에 따라 쳐막기와 걷어막기 등의 형태로 구성할 수 있으며, 음악과 조화롭게 속도의 변화를 주어 자유품새의 표현방법을 더욱 다양화 시킬 수 있다.

2) Hand techniques composition method

Each Poom is created with a technical system of Taekwondo movements that defend from and attack against an imagined opponent.

The target areas are divided into the very low, low, middle, high and very high sections. If the imagined opponent is attacking the middle area, the individual starts the Poom with a middle defensive technique before continuing to other techniques. If the imagined opponent attacks high, then the Poom starts with a high defensive technique.

The offensive and defensive techniques of each Poom are decided based on the section of the opponent's body that is being targeted (very low to very high).

Furthermore, blocks can take on various shapes and forms, such as counter and deflecting blocks. Additionally, the speed of each hand technique can be modified to fit with the music, creating countless ways to express different Freestyle Poomsae.

2.Taekwondo Basic Techniques

(1) 쳐막기 형태의 방어 + 공격
(1) Defensive Counter Blocks + Attacks

예시1] 안막기(중단) + 올려막기(상단) + 두 번지르기(중단, 상단) [방+방+공]

Example 1] Inward block (middle) + upward block (high) + 2 punches (middle, high) [defense + defense + attack]

2. 태권도 기본기술

예시2] 돌려지르기(상단) + 내려지르기(하단) + 아금손목치기(상단) [공+공+공]
Example 2] Turning punch (high) + downward punch (low) + arc hand strike (high)
[attack + attack + attack]

2. Taekwondo Basic Techniques

예시3] 당겨지르기(상단) + 금강막기+ 손날목치기(상단) [공+방+공]
Example 3] Pulling punch (high) + diamond block + knife hand neck strike (high)
[attack + defense + attack]

예시4] 눌러막기 + 손끝찌르기+ 표적팔굽치기(상단) [방+공+공]
Example 4] Pulling punch (high) + diamond block + knife hand neck strike (high)
[defense + attack + attack]

(2) 걷어막기 형태의 방어 + 공격
(2) Deflecting Types of Defensive Techniques + Attacks

쳐막기와 달리 상대의 공격을 최소한의 힘으로 흘려보내듯이 걷어내며 공방을 이어 갈 수 있다. 부드럽고 강한 동작을 표현하게 된다.

Unlike counter blocks, deflective blocks use minimal force to gently deflect away attacks, allowing for a flowing continuation of techniques.

Techniques can be expressed in both a strong and gentle manner.

예시1] 내려막기(중단) + 손날안치기(상단) + 손날바깥치기(상단)
[방+공+공]

Example 1] Downward block (middle) + inward knife hand strike (high) + backward knife hand strike (high) [defense + attack + attack]

2. Taekwondo Basic Techniques

예시2] 바깥막기(중단) + 숙여피하기 + 옆지르기 (상단)

[방+방+공]

Example 2] Outward Block (middle) + duck + side punch (high)
[defense + defense + attack]

예시3] 바탕손막기(중단) + 얼굴막기(상단) + 세워지르기(중단) [방+방+공]

Example 3] Palm Hand Block (middle) + Upward Block (high) + Upright Punch (middle)
[attack + defense + attack]

(3) 속도 및 리듬의 변화에 따른 동작 구성

2~3가지 동작으로 한 품을 엮어 속도와 리듬을 달리하여 공방을 이어 갈 수 있다.
경쾌하고 역동적인 동작을 표현하게 된다.

(3) Composition based on the Speed and Rhythm of the Techniques

A single Poom can have 2~3 techniques that are combined using a variety of different speeds and rhythms. This creates a nimble and dynamic kind of expression.

예시1] 몸통지르기(빠르게) + 등주먹치기(빠르게) + 손날막기(느리게)
Example 1] Middle punch (fast) + Back fist (fast) + knife hand block (slow)

2.Taekwondo Basic Techniques

예시2] 몸통안막기(빠르게) + 바깥막기(빠르게) + 손날막기(느리게)

Example 2] Inward middle block (fast) + outward block (fast) + knife hand block (slow)

3) 발기술

품새의 차기는 앞차기, 돌려차기, 옆차기 등으로 구성되고 목표점을 정확히 차는 형태를 표현해야 한다. 이에 반해 겨루기의 차기는 무릎을 빠르게 접어서 차며, 다음 동작을 빠르게 연결해 나아가야 한다.

이처럼 다양한 형태의 여러 가지 공격기술을 표현할 수 있어야 하고, 표현방법을 각 특성에 맞게 차기 구성을 해야 한다.

모든 차기는 정확한 목표와 과정이 표현되어야 한다.

3) Foot Techniques

Poomsae kicking techniques include front kicks, roundhouse kicks, side kicks, etc. In Kyorugi, kicks are quickly snapped back by bending the knee, then immediately followed by the next movement. However, in Poomsae, kicks must demonstrate proper execution with proper posture.

This is why a wide variety of attacking techniques must be demonstrated in a range of different manners in Poomsae, with each technique matched appropriately to the kicking style being demonstrated.

Regardless of the style of the kick being demonstrated, each one has a specific goal and method of execution.

2.Taekwondo Basic Techniques

(1) 공격기술 - 차기

상대방을 발로 가격하여 제압하기 위한 기술로서 무릎을 굽히거나 펴는 힘 또는 다리를 휘두르는 힘으로 공격하는 기술이다.

(1) Attacking Techniques – Kicks

Kicking techniques use the power of bending and straightening the knee and swinging the leg to attack and subdue opponents using foot strikes.

[끌어차기]

[Drag Kick]

[돌개차기]

[Tornado kick]

2. 태권도 기본기술

[돌개차기] / [Tornado Kick]

[두발당성차기] / [Double Kick]

[뒤차기] / [Back Kick]　　　　[밀어차기] / [Push Kick]

[바깥차기] / [Outward Crescent Kick]

2. Taekwondo Basic Techniques

[발걸고 짓찧기]

[Stamping Kick with Hooking the foot]

[발붙여 차기]

[Skipping Kick]

[비틀어차기]

[Twisted Kick]

2. 태권도 기본기술

[안차기]

[Inward Crescent Kick]

[짓찧기]

[Stamping Kick]

[표적바깥차기]   [표적안차기]   [후려차기]

[Outward Target Kick]   [Inward Target Kick]   [Whipping Kick]

4) 발기술 구성방법

자유품새는 공인품새에 비해 차기의 빈도수가 많으며 기술력의 채점항목은 다섯가지 형태의 차기기술이 포함된다.

필수 기술에 해당하는 항목 외에 발기술을 구성할 때는 거듭차기와 섞어차기 등이 주로 활용된다.

4) Composition Methods with Foot Techniques

There are generally more kicks in Freestyle Poomsae than there are in Recognized Poomsae, and the scoring criteria include five different elements that require kicks in technical skills category.

When foot techniques other than the required the techniques are included in Freestyle Poomsae, repeating kicks and combination kicks are typically used.

2. 태권도 기본기술

(1) 거듭차기

동일한 차기를 높이에 따른 변화를 주며 응용한다. (높이 - 최하단, 하단, 중단, 상단, 최상단)

(1) Repeating Kick

The same kick is demonstrated repeatedly at varying heights (heights - very low, low, middle, high, very high).

예시1] 거듭앞차기 = 앞차기(하단) + 앞차기(상단)

Example 1] Repeating front kick = front kick (low) + front kick (high)

예시2] 거듭돌려차기 = 돌려차기(하단) + 돌려차기(상단)

Example 2] Repeating roundhouse kick = roundhouse kick (low) + roundhouse kick (high)

2. Taekwondo Basic Techniques

예시3] 거듭옆차기 = 옆차기(하단) + 옆차기(상단)
Example 3] Repeating Side Kick = side kick (low) + side kick (high)

예시4] 옆차기3단계 = 옆차기(하단) + 옆차기(중단) + 옆차기(상단)
Example 4] 3-step Side Kick = side kick (low) + side kick (middle) + side kick (high)

2. 태권도 기본기술

(2) 섞어차기

다양한 차기를 섞어서 높이에 따른 변화를 주며 응용한다.

(2) Combination Kick

A variety of different kicks are combined and demonstrated varying heights.

예시1] 앞차기(중단)+돌려차기(중단)+거듭옆차기3단계(하단,중단,상단)
Example 1] Front kick (middle) + Roundhouse kick (middle) + Repeating Side Kick (low, middle, high)

2.Taekwondo Basic Techniques

(3) 속도 및 리듬에 따른 동작 구성

2~3가지 거듭차기와 섞어 차기에 속도 변화를 주어 더욱 난이도 있는 기술을 표현 할 수 있다.

(3) Composition of Movements based on the Speed and Rhythm

The speed of 2~3 repeating kicks and combination kicks can be varied to demonstrate more advanced techniques.

예시1] 앞차기(상단/5초) + 돌려차기(하단) + 돌려차기(중단) + 옆차기(상단)

Example 1] Front Kick (high/5 seconds) + roundhouse kick (low) + roundhouse kick (middle) + side kick (high)

5) 서기 및 딛기

서기란 자신의 체중을 지탱하여 서있는 상태로 태권도동작을 연결하기 위해 필요한 자세이다.

딛기란 상대방과의 거리 조절 및 공격과 방어동작 수행을 위해, 발을 여러 곳으로 움직이거나 방향을 바꾸는 동작이다.

품새 및 겨루기에서 이루어지는 발의 모든 움직임을 딛기라 표현한다.

5) Stances and Footworks

Stances are used to connect different taekwondo techniques while standing and supporting one's own body weight.

Footworks are used to control the distance from an opponent by moving the feet to different locations or using them to change directions.

All foot movements in Poomsae and Sparring are called 'Ditgi'.

2.Taekwondo Basic Techniques

(1) 서기

공격이나 방어기술을 수행하기 위해 지면을 발로 지탱하여 서있는 자세이다.

몸의 중심 이동과 방향 전환을 효율적으로 수행하기위해 지면을 발로 지탱하는 자세이다.

(1) Stances

A standing posture with feet on the ground is used to perform offensive and defensive techniques.

These postures support the body using the feet to shift one's center of gravity and efficiently change directions.

[앞서기] [Walking Stance]   [앞굽이] [Forward Stance]   [뒷굽이] [Back Stance]

[범서기] [Tiger Stance]   [앞꼬아서기] [Forward Cross Stance]   [뒤꼬아서기] [Back Cross Stance]

2. 태권도 기본기술

[주춤서기]

[Horse Riding Stance]

[곁다리서기]

[Assisting Stance]

[모서기]

[Diagonal Stance]

[학다리서기]

[Crane Stance]

6) 서기 및 딛기 구성방법

자유품새의 동선은 서기와 딛기로 구성할 수 있다.

다양한 서기와 딛기의 변화는 자유품새의 표현, 리듬에 중요한 역할을 한다.

음악과 조화롭게 움직일 수 있도록 구성해야 하며, 또한 동작이 자연스럽게 연결될 수 있도록 해준다.

6) Composition Method with Stances and Footworks

The line of motion in Freestyle Poomsae is composed of stances footwork.

Combining different stances and footwork play and important role in the expression and rhythm of Freestyle Poomsae.

Freestyle Poomsae should be choreographed in harmony with the music, with techniques naturally flowing between each other.

2. 태권도 기본기술

(1) 서기와 딛기의 연결구성

두 가지 서기자세의 중간에 딛기를 구성하여 동선의 변화를 준다.

(1) Connecting Stances and Footwork

The line of movements can be changed by inserting footwork between two stances.

예시1] 앞굽이 + 돌아딛기 + 뒷굽이

Example 1] Forward stance + turning step + back stance

예시2] 뒷굽이 + 물러딛기 + 학다리서기

Example 2] Back stance + backward step + crane stance

2. Taekwondo Basic Techniques

예시3] 범서기 + 옆딛기 + 주춤서기
Example 3] Tiger stance + side step + horse riding stance

예시4] 주춤서기 + 모딛기 + 뒷굽이
Example 4] Horse riding stance + diagonal step + back stance

2. 태권도 기본기술

7) 특수동작

공격과 방어기술을 효과적으로 수행하기 위한 일종의 예비동작으로 주로 사물의 모습을 모방하고 형상화한 동작이다.

이러한 특수동작은 자유품새에서 호흡을 조절하며 기운을 모으기 위해 주로 활용되며 음악과 조화를 더욱 효과적으로 표현할 수 있는 방법이다.

특수동작은 창작자의 의도와 목적에 따라 자유롭게 만들 수 있다.

7) Special Techniques

To perform offensive and defensive techniques effectively, these are preparation types of movements that mostly mirror objects to mimic their appearance.

These special techniques help control breathing and gather energy in Freestyle Poomsae and are also a way to harmonize with and express the accompanying music more effectively.

Special techniques can be freely created according to the intention and purposes of the creator.

[날개펴기]

[Wing Spreading]

[돌쩌귀]

[Hinge]

[밀어내기]

[Pushing]

2. Taekwondo Basic Techniques

[바위밀기]	[태산밀기]	[통밀기]

[Rock Push]	[Big Mountain Push]	[Log Push]

참고문헌

- 국기원태권도연구소(2019). 태권도용어사전. 도서출판 다락

3

자유품새의 필수기술

3. Mandatory techniques in Freestyle Poomsae

3 자유품새의 응용 기술
Application Techniques of Freestyle Poomsae

1) 뛰어 옆차기 Jumping Sidekick

2) 뛰어 앞차기 Multiple Front Kicks in a Jump

3) 회전 발차기 Gradient of Spins in a Spin Kick

4) 연속 발차기 Kyorugi Style Consecutive Kicking

5) 아크로바틱 Acrobatics

6) 뒤공중 Backflip

7) 모돌개차기 B-twist Kick

8) 휘돌개차기 Corkscrew Kick

9) 옆돌아 돌개차기 Cartwheel Full Twist Kick

10) 짚기 Scoot - Touch Down Rise

11) 기술 강화 훈련 Skill - Enhancement Training

12) 기술 차기의 응용 Variation of Kick

3.Application techniques of Freestyle Poomsae

1) 뛰어 옆차기

뛰어 옆차기는 높이 또는 멀리 있는 목표물을 한 발로 뛰어 올라 옆차기로 공격하는 기술이다.

자유품새 필수 기술 중 첫번째로 시연해야 하는 기술로써 세계태권도연맹에서는 차는발과 보조발의 중간높이로 평가하고 있다. 뛰어 옆차기의 완성도를 향상시키기 위해서는 높은 도약과 옆차기의 숙련성이 필요하다.

1) Jumping Side Kick

To demonstrate a jumping side kick, one foot is used to jump off and attack a target with a side kick. The jumping side kick should be high or far.

Jumping side kick is the first technique that must be demonstrated in Freestyle Poomsae. This technique is evaluated based on the height of the kick.

A perfectly executed technique will have both a high jump and an well executed side kick.

▶ 뛰어 옆차기
▶ Jumping Side Kick

3. 자유품새의 필수기술

단계별 기술 훈련

(1) 뛰어 옆차기 〈지면〉

뛰어 옆차기를 지면에 앉아 훈련하는 단계로 공중에서 필요한 자세를 연습한다.

1. 바닥에 앉아 다리를 모으고 한 손은 바닥을 짚어 몸을 지탱한다. 이때 무릎을 모으고, 어깨너 머로 시선 처리를 하며 옆차기 준비 자세를 취한다.

2. 옆차기를 찰때, 차는 발은 발 날을 만든다. 그리고 반대 발은 반대방향으로 당겨주어 완성도 높은 옆차기의 형태를 만든다.

3. 차는 발이 지면을 닿지 않도록 주의한다.

Step-by-Step Skill Training

(1) Jumping Side Kick <Ground>

In this step, you will practice your jumping side kick by practicing the posture you need to have in the air while sitting on the ground.

1. Sit on the floor with your legs together, and put one hand on the floor to help support your body.

2. From this position, bring your knees together. Look over the shoulder that is closer to your target and prepare to do a side kick.

3. The foot of your kicking leg should not touch the ground.

▶ 뛰어 옆차기 〈지면〉
▶ Jumping Side Kick 〈Ground〉

3.Application techniques of Freestyle Poomsae

단계별 기술 훈련

(2) 뛰어 옆차기 〈공중〉

1-1 '뛰어 옆차기 <지면>' 단계를 공중에서 연습한다. 공중에서의 옆차기를 실질적으로 시연하는 방법을 연습하는 단계이다.

1. 손으로 보조기구를 가볍게 짚고 도약을 준비한다.

2. 한 팔로 버팀과 동시에 뛰어 옆차기를 찬다. 이때 1-1. '뛰어 옆차기 <지면>' 단계에서 연습했던 발날과 몸의 균형에 집중한다.

3. 공중에서 옆차기를 차고 난 후 무릎을 몸쪽으로 당겨주며 착지한다.

Step-by-Step Skill Training

(2) Jumping Side Kick <Air>

In this step, the previous step, 1-1 'Jumping Side Kick <Ground>', is practiced in the air. In this step, actually demonstrating a side kick in the air is practiced.

1. Prepare to take off into the air with your hand lightly placed on top of assistive equipment.

2. Jump and do a side kick while lightly supporting yourself with one arm.

3. After doing your side kick in the air, pull your knee back in towards your body as you land.

▶ 뛰어 옆차기 〈공중〉
▶ Jumping Side Kick 〈Air〉

3. 자유품새의 필수기술

단계별 기술 훈련

(3) 뛰어 옆차기 〈자세〉

뛰어 옆차기의 올바른 표현을 위해 '자세'를 훈련한다.

1. 차는 발을 옆차기 차기 전의 자세를 유지하고 준비한다.
2. 자세를 유지하며 하나, 둘, 셋 구령에 맞추어 한 발로 가볍게 뛰어간다.
3. 세번째 도약에서 발을 접어 모아주며 뛰어 옆차기 공중 자세를 만들며 반복한다.

Step-by-Step Skill Training

(3) Jumping Side Kick <Posture>

In this step, you will practice the correct posture for your jumping side kick.

1. Make sure you are in the right posture before starting your side kick.
2. Lightly run forward with a 1, 2, 3 count, while maintaining your posture.
3. On the count of '3', jump as you gather your feet together to form a side kick posture in the air. Practice by repeating these steps.

▶ 뛰어 옆차기 〈자세〉
▶ Jumping Side Kick <Posture>

3.Application techniques of Freestyle Poomsae

단계별 기술 훈련

(4) 뛰어 옆차기 〈도약〉

도움닫기를 통해 뛰어 옆차기 공중 자세를 훈련한다.

1. 옆차기의 발날을 만들고 무릎을 모아 도약과 동시에 보조발을 힘껏 끌어올려 다리를 모아준다.
2. 이때 주의해야 할 점은 보조발의 뒤꿈치만 올리지 않고, 보조발의 안쪽 전체가 올라올 수 있도록 한다.
3. 공중에서 뛰어 옆차기를 차기 전의 자세를 만들어주며, 양발은 지면과 수평으로 모아주고 양손은 가슴에 모아준다.

Step-by-Step Skill Training

(4) Jumping Side Kick <Jump>

In this step, you will practice your midair jumping side kick form by focusing on run up.

1. Create the proper foot position needed for a jumping side kick with the blade of your kicking foot. At the same time, bring both knees together and pull up your supporting leg with as much power as you can.

2. During this step, it is important to make sure that you are raising the entire inner area of your supporting foot, and not just your heel.

3. While you are in the air, create the proper jumping side kick posture before kicking. Your feet should both be parallel to the ground, and your hands gathered close to your chest.

▶ 뛰어 옆차기 〈도약〉
▶ Jumping Side Kick 〈Jump〉

단계별 기술 훈련

(5) 뛰어 옆차기

이전 훈련 과정을 기억하며 뛰어 옆차기를 수행한다.

도움닫기 시 속도가 빨라지도록 하고, 차기 후에 균형을 유지한다.

1. 뛰어 옆차기는 찬 높이를 평가 받기 때문에 자신이 발휘할 수 있는 최고 높이로 찬다.
2. 뛰어 옆차기의 완성도를 위해 보조발을 끌어 올리며, 양팔을 몸쪽으로 유지한다.
3. 착지 시 부상 방지를 위해 중심을 유지하며, 양 발이 차례로 떨어지도록 한다.

Step-by-Step Skill Training

(5) Jumping Side Kick

Remembering what you practiced in the previous steps, practice your jumping side kick.

Increase the speed of the movements during run up, and stay balanced after the kick.

1. The jumping side kick is scored based on the height of the kick, so try to kick as high as you can.
2. To perfect your jumping side kick, Pull in your supporting leg and both arms towards your body.
3. To prevent injuries when landing, keep your balance and let your feet fall back to the ground one after the other.

▶ 뛰어 옆차기
▶ Jumping Side Kick

3.Application techniques of Freestyle Poomsae

2) 뛰어 앞차기

뛰어 앞차기는 높이 또는 멀리 있는 목표물을 한 발로 뛰어 올라 앞차기로 여러번 공격하는 기술이다.

자유품새 필수 기술 중 두 번째로 시연해야 하는 기술로써 '차기의 횟수'를 평가한다.

허리 이상 차는 것을 규정으로 하며, 차기는 무릎을 기준으로 90° 이상 접었다 펴야한다.

2) Multiple Front Kicks in a Jump

To demonstrate multiple kicks in a jump, a person jumps with one foot to attack a target that is either high or far away, multiple times with front kicks.

Multiple kicks in a jump is the second technique that must be demonstrated in Freestyle Poomsae. This technique is evaluated on the 'number of kicks' that are demonstrated.

In order to be scored, each kick must be above the waist, and folded and unfolded at least 90° from the knee.

▶ 뛰어 앞차기
▶ Multiple front kicks in a jump

3. 자유품새의 필수기술

단계별 기술 훈련

(1) 번갈아 앞차기

공중에서 수행하는 연속 앞차기의 구분 동작을 지면에서 번갈아 차는 훈련이다. 공중에서 정확하고 빠르게 차는 기능을 향상 시킬 수 있다.

1. 보조자와 마주 본 상태에서 시연자는 한 발의 무릎을 90°로 들고 준비한다. 이후 구령에 맞추어 발을 교차하며 앞차기를 찬다. 타겟의 높이는 명치 높이로 하고, 보조 발의 무릎이 내려가지 않도록 한다.

2. 차기의 표현성과 속도를 위해 발목을 피고 앞차기를 차고, 양 발을 교차하며 차도록 한다.

Step-by-Step Skill Training

(1) Switching Front Kick

In this step, a consecutive series of front kicks that will be done in the air are broken down and practiced on the ground. This can perfect the ability to kick in the air both quickly and accurately.

1. Standing face-to-face with a partner, lift one knee up to a 90° angle. On your count, switch feet and do a front kick. The height of the target should be at the height of your chest, and the knee of the supporting leg should not be brought down.

2. For the expression of energy and speed of the kick, straighten the angle when kicking, and switch between your legs for each kick.

▶ 번갈아 앞차기
▶ Switching Front Kick

3.Application techniques of Freestyle Poomsae

단계별 기술 훈련

(2) 도약발 앞차기

뛰어 앞차기의 체공을 향상시키기 위한 훈련이다.

1. 시작 자세는 2-1. 뛰어 앞차기 <번갈아 앞차기>와 동일하며, 오른발 잡이는 왼발로 도약 훈련을 한다. 타겟의 높이는 시연자의 허리 높이로 한다.

2. 같은 발로 도약, 차기, 착지를 모두 수행한다. 안정적인 착지를 위해서 차기를 빠르게 차고 접도록 한다.

Step-by-Step Skill Training

(2) Front Kick with the Jumping leg

In this step, you will practice holding the position for jumping front kick.

1. The starting position is identical to that of the previous step, '2-1 Switching Front Kick'. If you have a dominant right leg, practice jumping with your left leg, and vice versa. The target's height should be at waist-level.

2. You should jump, kick, and land with the same leg. For a safe landing, straighten and bend your kicking leg quickly.

▶ 도약발 앞차기
▶ Leaping Front Kick

단계별 기술 훈련

(3) 연속 차기

1. 시연자는 보조자와 마주한 채로 지면에 누워 무릎을 들어 올리고, 보조자는 앞굽이의 형태로 타겟을 잡는다.

2. 무릎을 고정한 채로 연속해서 앞차기 3~5회를 빠르게 찬다. 차고 난 후 두발을 모아 착지에 대한 훈련을 같이 한다.

3. 보조자는 시연자의 무릎의 각도와 맞춰 타겟을 잡아주어 차기의 가동범위를 크게한다.

Step-by-Step Skill Training

(3) Consecutive Kicks

1. Have a partner hold a target in front of you in a forward stance. Facing your helper, sit back on the ground with your knees raised up.

2. Making sure to keep your knees still, quickly throw 3~5 kicks in succession. After finishing the consecutive kicks, bring both feet next to each other. Practicing bringing your feet together after finishing your kicks will help you practice the position they should be in for landing.

3. Your partner can increase the range of motion of your kicks by holding the target higher or lower. The angle and location of the target should be decided by following the extension of your legs from your knees.

▶ 연속차기
▶ Consecutive kicks

3.Application techniques of Freestyle Poomsae

단계별 기술 훈련

(4) 뛰어 앞차기 〈정확성〉

공중에서 무릎 올리기를 통해 차기의 높이와 정확성을 향상시키기 위한 훈련이다.

1. 1-4. '뛰어 옆차기 〈도약〉'의 연습과 동일하게 도약을 한다.

2. 시연자의 신체 능력에 맞추어 3~5회까지 허리이상의 높이로 무릎을 교차하여 수행한다.

3. 착지 시 부상 방지를 위해 중심을 유지하며, 양 발이 차례로 떨어지도록 한다.

Step-by-Step Skill Training

(4) Jumping Front Kick <Accuracy>

In this step, you will improve the height and accuracy of your jumping front kick by practicing raising your knee in the air.

1. Jump in the same way you practiced in section '1-4 Jumping Side Kick <Run up>'.

2. Bring one knee up above your waist, then switch knees. Depending on your skill level, raise your knees 3~5 times in the air, alternating between your legs.

3. To avoid injuring yourself when landing, maintain your balance and let your feet fall back to the ground one at a time.

▶ 뛰어 앞차기 〈정확성〉
▶ Jumping Front Kick 〈Accuracy〉

3. 자유품새의 필수기술

단계별 기술 훈련

(5) 뛰어 앞차기 3~5단계

2-4의 '뛰어 앞차기 <정확성>'에서 수행했던 무릎 올리기를 시연자의 능력에 맞추어 3~5회 찬다.

1. 차기 속도에 집중하여 여러 번 찬다.
2. 허리 높이 이상으로 차기를 구사한다.

Step-by-Step Skill Training

(5) Jumping Front Kick Steps 3~5

Just like you practiced in the previous step, '2-4 Jumping Front Kick <Accuracy>', raise your knees 3~5 times, according to your skill level.

1. Kick as many times as you are able, focusing on the speed of your kicks.
2. Make sure that you are kicking above your waist.

▶ 뛰어 앞차기 3~5단계
▶ Jumping Front Kick Steps 3~5

3.Application techniques of Freestyle Poomsae

3) 회전 발차기

회전 발차기는 앞 발을 중심으로 몸을 회전하여 목표물을 돌려차기 또는 후려차기로 공격하는 기술이다.

자유품새 필수 기술 중 세 번째로 시연해야 하는 기술로써 중심이 되는 발을 기준으로 하여 '회전각'을 평가받는다.

대표적으로 540° 뒤후려차기, 720° 돌개차기, 900° 뒤후려차기 등이 있다.

3) Gradient of Spins in a Spin Kick

To demonstrate the gradient of spins in a spin kick, the body spins using the front leg as a rotation axis, attacking a target with roundhouse kicks and hook kicks.

Gradient of spins in a spin kick is the third technique that must be demonstrated in Freestyle Poomsae. This technique is evaluated on the 'degree of rotation' of the central foot.

Representative techniques include the 540° spinning hook kick, 720° roundhouse kick, and 900° spinning hook kick

▶ 회전 발차기
▶ Spin Kick

3. 자유품새의 필수기술

단계별 기술 훈련

(1) 540° 뒤후려차기 〈회전축 연습〉

'회전발'은 회전을 위해 체중을 싣는 발을 말한다. 더 많은 회전각을 위해 회전축을 안정적으로 만드는 훈련이다.

1. 회전발을 앞으로 디딘 자세에서 한 바퀴 회전을 한다. 양팔을 회전 반대 방향으로 가볍게 돌리며 회전을 시작한다.

2. 회전을 시작할 때 시선을 정면으로 고정한다.

3. 회전 후 착지는 시작과 동일한 위치와 자세를 만들어 준다.

Step-by-Step Skill Training

(1) 540° Spining Hook Kick <Training a Stable Rotational Axis>

Your 'rotating leg' is the leg supporting your body weight as you rotate. In this step, you will increase the stability of your central rotation axis for different rotation angles.

1. Standing with your rotating leg forward, make one full rotation. Before starting the rotation, wind up both your arms in the direction that is opposite your turn.

2. Keep your eyes fixed straight ahead when you are starting your rotation.

3. When you land after the rotation, your body should be in the same position and posture it was in before the rotation.

▶ 540° 뒤후려차기 〈회전축 연습〉
▶ 540° Spining Hook Kick
  〈Training a Stable Rotational Axis〉

3.Application techniques of Freestyle Poomsae

단계별 기술 훈련

(2) 돌개차기

회전 발차기의 가장 기본이 되는 차기이다. 회전축이 안정된 상태에서 훈련해야 효과적이다.

1. 회전발을 앞으로 내딛고 몸은 옆으로 틀어 선다. 보조발과 양팔을 함께 들어 올리며 회전을 한다.
2. 회전 중 시선은 정면을 유지하여 회전의 중심을 잡아준다.
3. 회전 시 보조발을 올리며 차기를 시작한다.

Step-by-Step Skill Training

(2) Tornado Kick

The tornado kick is the most basic of all the spinning kicks. If you want your training to be efficient, you should only start practicing this kick after developing a stable rotation axis as outlined in the previous step.

1. With your rotating leg forward, stand with your body turned to the side. Lift both arms and your supporting leg up and rotate.
2. As you rotate, keep your balance by fixing your gaze straight ahead of you.
3. During your rotation, raise your supporting leg to start your kick.

▶ 돌개차기
▶ Tornado Kick

3. 자유품새의 필수기술

단계별 기술 훈련

(3) 540° 뒤후려차기 〈시선〉

충분한 회전각을 표현하기 위해 시선을 보는 방법이다.

1. 회전 발을 앞으로 디딘 후 3-1. 540° 뒤후려차기 <회전축>과정과 3-2. 540° 뒤후려차기 <돌개차기>과정을 더해 540° 회전을 한다.

2. 시선은 정면으로 세 번 확인한다. 첫번째는 준비 서기, 두 번째는 한 바퀴 회전 후 도약하는 순간, 세 번 째는후려차기 전이다.

3. 착지 시 뒤후려차기의 예비동작을 만들어야 한다.

Step-by-Step Skill Training

(3) 540° Spinning Hook Kick <Gaze>

Being able to control where you are looking is important for being comfortable with different rotation angles.

1. Take one step forward with your rotating leg. Rotate 540° by combining step '3-1 Developing a Stable Rotation Axis' with step '3-2. Tornado Kick'.

2. There are three moments when you should be looking forwards. First, in your ready position; second, after your first rotation, when you start taking off for your jump; third, before your hook kick.

3. Prepare the chamber for your hook kick as you land.

▶ 540° 뒤후려차기 〈시선〉
▶ 540° Spining Hook Kick〈Gaze〉

3.Application techniques of Freestyle Poomsae

단계별 기술 훈련

(4) 540° 뒤후려차기

1. 중심이 되는 발을 뒤로 한 상태에서 한걸음 나가며 540° 뒤후려차기를 찬다.
2. 한걸음 앞으로 나갈 때 몸과 함께 앞발을 회전 방향으로 돌린다.
3. 뒷발은 진행 방향으로 밀어주어 동작의 가속을 더한다.
4. 뒤후려차기 시 어깨를 닫는다.

Step-by-Step Skill Training

(4) 540° Spinning Hook Kick

1. Stand with your rotating foot in the back, then take one step forward and do a 540° hook kick.
2. As you take a step forward, your front leg should turn in the same direction your body is moving.
3. Push off the ground with your back leg in the direction your body is turning to accelerate your movement.
4. Close off your shoulders as you kick.

▶ 540° 뒤후려차기
▶ 540° Spinning hook Kick

3. 자유품새의 필수기술

단계별 기술 훈련

(5) 720° 돌개차기 〈회전 자세〉

1. 몸을 꼬아 서서 양 팔과 보조 발을 들어 올리며 한 바퀴 회전을 한다.
2. 가볍게 뛰는 동시에 양 팔을 회전 방향쪽으로 당기며 한 바퀴 회전을 한다.
3. 회전 시 회전축을 수직으로 유지한다.

Step-by-Step Skill Training

(5) 720° Roundhouse Kick <Rotating Position>

1. Stand with your legs crossed and your body twisted. Raising both arms and your supporting leg, do one Full spin.
2. As you lightly jump up, simultaneously pull in your arms in the same direction you are rotating, and do one Full spin.
3. Keep your rotation axis vertical during your rotation.

▶ 720° 돌개차기 〈회전 자세〉
▶ 720° Tornado Kick 〈Rotating Position〉

3.Application Techniques of Freestyle Poomsae

단계별 기술 훈련

(6) 720° 돌개차기 〈회전각〉

1. 3-1. 540° 뒤후려차기 〈회전축 연습〉 동작 후, 양팔과 보조 발을 동시에 돌리며 회전한다.
2. 뛰는 동시에 3-5. '720° 돌개차기 〈회전 자세〉'에서 연습했던 회전각을 만들어 주며 추가로 회전을 진행하고 착지한다. 이때 보조 발 무릎의 시작과 끝의 높이가 떨어지지 않게 한다.
3. 두발이 동시에 착지 하도록 하고, 보조발이 몸 뒤쪽으로 올수 있도록 한다.

Step-by-Step Skill Training

(6) 720° Roundhouse Kick <Gradient angle>

1. After doing the 'rotation axis' motion as described in step '3-1', turn using both arms and your supporting leg.
2. As you jump, use the same movements that you practiced in step '3-5, 720° Roundhouse Kick <Turning Position>'. Keep the same rotation angle but add one extra rotation to your jump before landing. The knee of your supporting leg should stay at the same height from the beginning to the end of your rotation.
3. Both feet should land at the same time, with the supporting leg landing towards the back of the body.

▶ 720° 돌개차기 〈회전각〉
▶ 720° Tornado Kick 〈Gradient Angle〉

3. 자유품새의 필수기술

단계별 기술 훈련

(7) 720° 돌개차기 〈착지〉

1. 3-6. '720° 돌개차기 〈회전각〉' 과정이 완성되면 회전이 끝나는 지점에서 발을 교차하며 착지한다.
2. 착지하는 동시에 들고 있는 무릎이 돌려차기를 찰 수 있도록 한다.

Step-by-Step Skill Training

(7) 720° Roundhouse Kick <Landing>

1. Do step '3-6, 720° Roundhouse Kick <Rotation Angle>', but switch feet as you land.
2. As you land, simultaneously execute a roundhouse kick with the leg that is holding a knee up.

▶ 720° 돌개차기 〈착지〉
▶ 720° Roundhouse Kick 〈Landing〉

3.Application techniques of Freestyle Poomsae

단계별 기술 훈련

(8) 720° 돌개차기

1. 한걸음 나가며 720° 돌개차기를 한다.
2. 한걸음 앞으로 나갈 때 몸과 함께 앞발을 회전 방향으로 돌린다.
3. 뒷발은 진행 방향으로 밀어주어 동작의 가속을 더한다.
4. 완전한 회전 후에 돌려차기를 한다.

Step-by-Step Skill Training

(8) 720° Roundhouse Kick

1. Take one step forward and do a 720° roundhouse kick.
2. As you take a step forward, your front leg should turn in the same direction your body is turning.
3. Push off the ground with your back leg in the direction your body is turning to accelerate your movement.
4. After completing a full rotation, execute a roundhouse kick.

▶ 720° 돌개차기
▶ 720° Roundhouse Kick

3. 자유품새의 필수기술

4) 연속발차기

연속발차기는 겨루기 형태의 딛기와 차기의 연결을 뜻한다. 자유품새 필수 기술 중 네 번 째로 시연해야 하는 기술로써 난이도와 정확도로 평가한다. 연결의 속성이 무한하여 대표적인 몇가지 예로 설명하기로 한다.

4) Kyorugi Style Consecutive Kicking

Kyorugi Style Consecutive kicks refers to the style of continuous stepping and kicking used in sparring.

Kyorugi style consecutive kicks are the fourth technique that must be demonstrated in Freestyle Poomsae.

This technique is evaluated on the level of complexity and accuracy of the kicks.

Since there are an infinite number of combinations that can be created, only several representative examples will be described here.

▶ 연속발차기
▶ Kyorugi Style Consecutive Kicking

3.Application techniques of Freestyle Poomsae

단계별 기술 훈련

(1) 나래차기

1. 첫발의 힘을 두번째 발에 비해 70~80% 정도로 하여 두번째 차기 시 허리 회전의 수월함을 높인다.
2. 차는 발의 무릎 방향을 사선으로 허리를 틀어 빠르게 연결한다.
3. 양 무릎이 벌어지지 않게 하여 연결 속도가 빠르게 이어지도록 한다.
4. 양발 교차 시 지면에 떨어지는 시간을 최소화 하여 앞으로 나아가며 찬다.

Step-by-Step Skill Training

(1) Double Roundhouse Kick

1. Your first kick should only have about 70~80% of the strength of your second kick. This will make it easier for you to rotate your hips for the second kick.
2. Quickly connect your kicks by turning your hips diagonally to the angle created by the direction the knee of your kicking leg is facing.
3. Making sure your knees do not spread apart from each other, this will help you kick multiple kicks quickly.
4. Move forward as you alternate legs to kick. This will minimize the time it takes for your legs to fall back down to the ground.

▶ 나래차기
▶ Double Roundhouse Kick

3. 자유품새의 필수기술

단계별 기술 훈련

(2) 상단 돌려차기

차기의 표현을 위해 상체가 앞으로 숙여지지 않도록 하고 무릎을 높이 올려 찬다.

1. 무릎과 무릎이 스치듯 사선으로 올려준다.
2. 발목을 곧게 펴주어 발 끝 선을 날카롭게 해준다.
3. 차기 시 허리와 골반을 사용하여 차기의 높이를 올리고 빠르게 차고 접는다.
4. 예시로는 앞발 제자리 상단 돌려차기, 발붙여 내려차기, 발붙여 돌려차기 등이 있다.

Step-by-Step Skill Training

(2) High Section Roundhouse Kick

For good presentation and expression of energy, bring your knee up high and keep your upper body from leaning too far forward.

1. Raise your knee up in a way that your knees brush past each other.
2. Straighten your ankles and make a sharp line upwards with the ends of your toes.
3. When kicking, use your hips and pelvis to raise your kick higher, making sure to kick and snap your leg back quickly.
4. For example, stationary front leg high section roundhouse kick, skipping axe kick, skipping roundhouse kick etc.

▶ 상단 돌려차기
▶ High Section Roundhouse Kick

3.Application techniques of Freestyle Poomsae

단계별 기술 훈련

(3) 돌개차기

빠르게 돌아 딛기를 하여 회전하고 길게 앞으로 나아가는 연습이 필요하다. 간결한 차기동작을 위해 양무릎 사이가 벌어지지않도록 한다.
1. 상체의 중심이동을 앞으로 하며 뒷발을 회전하여 무릎을 올린다.
2. 회전 후 축이 되는 발을 가볍게 튕겨주며 앞으로 나아갈 수 있는 힘을 만든다.
3. 차기 동작이 크게 돌아가지 않도록 간결한 무릎 모양을 만든다.
4. 차기를 빠르게 차고 접어준다.
5. 몸의 중심을 낮추어 진행하고, 길고 빠르게 찬다.

Step-by-Step Skill Training

(3) Kyorugi Style Tornado Kick

For this technique, practice taking a quick turning step that covers a lot of ground forwards. To keep your kicking motion quick, your knees should not spread apart form each other.
1. Shift your body's centre of gravity forward while turning your back foot and bringing your knee up.
2. After your rotation, create some forward momentum by lightly bouncing the foot of the leg that is your rotation axis.
3. Tightly bend your knee so your kicking motion does not become too large.
4. Quickly kick and snap back your leg.
5. As you practice, lower your centre of gravity, kick with a long reach, and kick quickly.

▶ 돌개차기
▶ Kyorugi Style Tornado Kick

3. 자유품새의 필수기술

단계별 기술 훈련

(4) 연속발차기 〈구성 예시〉

1. 발붙여차기 - 돌려차기 - 나래차기 - 돌개차기 - 뒷차기
2. 발붙여차기 - 앞발 나래차기 - 발붙여 내려차기 - 돌개차기 - 후려차기
3. 발붙여 나래차기 - 돌개차기 - 뒷차기 - 물러딛고 폼바꾼 후 후려차기

Step-by-Step Skill Training

(4) Kyorugi Style Consecutive Kicks <Examples>

1. Skipping kick – roundhouse kick – double roundhouse kick – tornado kick – back kick
2. Skipping kick – front leg double roundhouse kick – skipping axe kick – tornado kick – spinning hook kick
3. Skipping double roundhouse kick – tornado kick – back kick – step back switch feet – spinning hook kick

▶ 연속발차기 〈구성 예시〉
▶ Kyorugi Style Consecutive Kicks 〈Examples〉

5) 아크로바틱

아크로바틱은 체조 경기에 사용되는 모든 아크로바틱 동작을 말하며 차기가 포함되어야 한다.

자유품새 필수 기술 중 마지막으로 시연해야 하는 기술로써 신체를 활용한 기술을 통해 '난이도'를 평가받는다.

안정적인 경기력을 위해서는 아크로바틱 기술수행에 대한 자신감이 필수 조건이다.

5) Acrobatics

Acrobatics in Freestyle Poomsae refers to movements used in gymnastics competitions, but with the inclusion of kicks.

Acrobatic kicking technique is the last technique that must be demonstrated in Freestyle Poomsae. It is evaluated on the level of technical difficulty of the techniques that are demonstrated.

Confidence is crucial for demonstrating a solid execution of acrobatic kicking techniques.

▶ 아크로바틱
▶ Acrobatics

3. 자유품새의 필수기술

단계별 기술 훈련

(1) 물구나무서기

1. 기술 발휘와 안정성을 위한 기초 단계이다.

2. 앞굽이의 형태에서 머리가 앞발 위로 올 수 있도록 중심을 앞으로 기울여 준다. 이때 팔을 귀에 붙여 상체 자세를 곧게 한다.

3. 벽에 기대어 물구나무서기를 하고, 온몸을 곧게 펴준다. 이때 시선은 바닥으로 향하고 어깨 및 상체가 굽지 않도록 주의 한다.

Step-by-Step Skill Training

(1) Handstand

1. This is a basic skill required for skill development and stability and acrobatics techniques.

2. From a forward stance, move your centre of gravity forwards so you can bring your head above your front leg. Place your arms directly beside your ears and straighten your upper body.

3. Do a handstand by leaning against a wall, and ensure your body is completely straight. Look at the floor and be sure to keep your body below the shoulders straight.

▶ 물구나무서기
▶ Handstand

3.Application techniques of Freestyle Poomsae

단계별 기술 훈련

(2) 물구나무서기 〈이동〉

1. 벽을 향해 측면에서 물구나무서기를 준비하고, 다리를 차올릴 때 손은 옆으로 틀어 벽과 마주하도록 물구나무서기를 한다.

2. 다리는 벌린 상태에서 양손에 체중을 번갈아 싣고 옆으로 이동한다.

3. 착지 시 한 손은 고정하고 반대 손은 방향을 틀고 옮겨 짚으며 착지한다.

Step-by-Step Skill Training

(2) Handstand <Moving>

1. Facing the wall, prepare to do a handstand. As you kick your feet up for a handstand, turn your hands sideways so they are parallel to the wall.

2. With your legs spread apart, shift your weight back and forth from hand to hand and move side to side.

3. To land back on your feet, move one hand by turning and planting it to the side, while keeping the other hand in its place.

▶ 물구나무서기 〈이동〉
▶ Handstand 〈Moving〉

단계별 기술 훈련

(3) 물구나무서기 〈착지〉

1. 5-2. '물구나무서기 〈이동〉' 과 시작은 동일하다. 다리를 모아 중심을 잡고, 방향 전환을 하며 두 발로 착지한다.

2. 착지 시 등을 최대한 빠르게 올린다. 이때 발이 지면에 닿고 손을 들며 몸이 구부러진 형태가 되지 않도록 주의한다.

Step-by-Step Skill Training

(3) Handstand <Landing>

1. Start as you would in step 5-2's 'Handstand <Moving>'. Bring your legs together and gather your balance, then land on both feet as you change directions.

2. When you land, straighten your back as quickly as you can. Make sure your hands are raised and your body is not bent at the moment your feet land on the ground again.

▶ 물구나무서기 〈착지〉
▶ Handstand 〈Landing〉

3.Application techniques of Freestyle Poomsae

단계별 기술 훈련

(4) 측전 〈시작〉

1. 측전 동작을 시작하기 위해 필요한 준비 과정으로 'hop step'으로 불린다.
2. 차렷한 자세에서 양팔을 흔들며 살짝 뛰어서 물구나무서기 준비 자세를 만든다.
3. 첫 번째 타겟에 첫발, 두 번째 타겟에 다음 발, 세 번째 타겟에 손을 짚으며 물구나무 서기만 가볍게 진행하고 돌아온다.

Step-by-Step Skill Training

(4) Roundoff <Start>

1. A preparatory motion often referred to as the 'hurdle' is needed to initiate a roundoff
2. Laying down on the floor, place targets at the locations of your feet, hips, and hands.
3. Lining up your first foot to the first target, your second foot to the second target, and your hands to the third target, do a handstand before returning to your original position.

▶ 측전 〈시작〉
▶ Roundoff 〈Start〉

3. 자유품새의 필수기술

단계별 기술 훈련

(5) 측전 〈진행〉

1. 5-4. '측전 <시작>' 과 동일하게 시작한다. 두 번째 손을 짚는 동시에 방향전환을 하여 올렸던 발을 그대로 착지한다.

2. 몸을 곧게 펴서 양 팔이 귀에 붙일 정도로 들어야 하며, 허리도 굽혀지지 않도록 한다. 착지할 때 몸이 틀어지지 않도록 하고, 시선은 양손의 가운데로 향하도록 한다.

Step-by-Step Skill Training

(5) Roundoff \<progression\>

1. Start as you did in step '5-4 Roundoff <Start>'. However, in the instant you put down your second hand, change directions and immediately lower your raised foot straight down to the ground.

2. Your body should be completely straight without bending at the waist, and your arms should be raised so that they are directly beside your ears. Do not twist your body as you land, and direct your gaze towards the middle of your two hands.

▶ 측전 〈진행〉
▶ Roundoff 〈progression〉

3.Application techniques of Freestyle Poomsae

단계별 기술 훈련

(6) 측전 〈착지〉

1. 양발을 최대한 빨리 모아 착지하고 점프를 살짝 뛴다.
2. 착지 시 자세가 5-3. '물구나무서기 <착지>' 와 마찬가지로 몸을 곧게 편다.

Step-by-Step Skill Training

(6) Roundoff <Landing>

1. When landing, bring your feet together as quickly as possible, then finish with a slight jump.
2. Just as you practiced in step '5-3 Handstand <Landing>', your body should be straight when you land.

▶ 측전 〈착지〉
▶ Roundoff 〈Landing〉

6) 뒤공중

뒤공중은 자유품새 필수기술 중 아크로바틱으로 포함 되는 기술이기 때문에 매우 중요하다. '백플립', '쭈가리'등 다양한 명칭으로 쓰이고 있지만 국기원 기술 용어 정립에 따라 뒤공중으로 통일하였다. 제자리에서 도약 후 뒤로 회전하는 동작이며, 태권도 시범에서 격파기술로도 오랫동안 사용되고 있다.

6) Backflip

Backflips are very important because they are included in Freestyle Poomsae's Mandatory Techniques, Acrobatics. Although it is called a variety of different names amongst Taekwondo athletes and coaches, the Kukkiwon's technical terms for it is 'Dwi-gong-joong (Backflip)'. For this movement, you rotate backwards after jumping up on the spot. The backflip has been used as a breaking technique in Taekwondo demonstrations.

Many different techniques have been derived from the backflip because it allows for a variety of different kicks to be demonstrated during it. Acrobatic Kicking Technique is the last required technique that must be demonstrated in Freestyle Poomsae, and the roundoff backflip with multiple kicks is a commonly used technique.

▶ 뒤공중
▶ Backflip

3.Application techniques of Freestyle Poomsae

단계별 기술 훈련

(1) 뒤공중 〈기초〉

공중에서 이루어 지는 뒤공중 동작을 지면에 누워서 안전하게 훈련하는 단계이다.

1. 뒤공중을 시작하는 단계로 지면에 누워 팔을 위로 들어준다.
2. 점프를 위한 단계로 손을 지면에 닿을 때까지 내리며 무릎을 구부린다.
3. 손을 위로 올리면서 다리를 편다.
4. 뒤공중 〈기초〉 단계의 핵심 동작으로 뒤구르기처럼 몸을 최대한 말아서 무릎을 끌어안는다.
5. 무릎이 어깨 위를 지나간다고 생각하며 몸을 말아주고, 손으로 무릎을 가슴 쪽으로 당겨준다.

Step-by-Step Skill Training

(1) Backflip <Basics>

In this step, we will practice a backflip motions while safely lying down on the ground.

1. To start, lie down on the ground on your back with your arms raised.
2. In preparation for the jump, bend your knees while lowering your arms until your hands touch the floor.
3. The key movement in this step is to curl up your body as tightly as possible, just as you would in a somersault.
4. Tightly curl up your body while imagining curling up your knees so tightly that they would pass over your shoulders. Use your hands to pull your knees tightly towards your chest.

▶ 뒤공중 〈기초〉
▶ Backflip 〈Basics〉

3. 자유품새의 필수기술

단계별 기술 훈련

(2) 뒤공중 〈도약〉

뒤공중 점프 훈련 단계로 올바른 도약과 회전을 연습할 수 있다.

1. 시연자는 제자리 점프를 준비하고, 보조자는 시연자의 옆에 서서 허리를 받치고 준비한다.

2. 6-1. '뒤공중 <기초>' 점프를 한다. 시연자는 상체를 많이 숙이지 말고 하체를 사용하여 뛰고, 보조자는 허리를 받쳐 올려주어 체공시간을 늘려준다.

3. 6-1. '뒤공중 <기초>' 과정과 동일하게 무릎을 어깨위로 올려준다. 이때 보조자는 시연자가 뒤로 넘어가지 않게 보조를 한다.

Step-by-Step Skill Training

(2) Backflip <Jump>

In this step, the correct form for jumping and rotating for a backflip will be practiced.

1. With a spotter standing beside you and supporting your waist, prepare to jump in place.

2. Jump as you practiced in the previous step, 6-1 'Backflip <Basics>'. Jump up using your lower body strength, and make sure not to bend your upper body too much. Your spotter should extend your airtime by lifting you and supporting you from your waist.

3. Tightly curl up your body just like you practiced in '6-1 Backflip <Basics>', while imagining tucking your knees so tightly into yourself that they would pass over your shoulders. As you do this, your spotter will make sure you do not fall backwards

▶ 측전 〈진행〉
▶ Roundoff 〈progression〉

3.Application techniques of Freestyle Poomsae

단계별 기술 훈련

(3) 뒤공중 〈말기〉

뒤공중의 공포심을 없애고 올바르게 몸을 마는 연습 단계이다.

1. 허리 이상 높이의 안전 매트를 두고 한걸음 앞에 선다.
2. 6-2. '뒤공중 <도약>' 와 동일하게 상체가 위로 곧게 올라가도록 한다. 점프 시 상체가 숙여 지거나 뒤로 눕지 않도록 한다.
3. 점프의 최고점에 다다르기 직전, 뒤구르기처럼 몸을 말아 자세를 유지하고 등으로 착지한다.

Step-by-Step Skill Training

(3) Backflip <Rolling>

This step will help you overcome any fears about the feeling of turning backwards in midair. It will also help you develop the proper rolling form.

1. Using safety mats at least as tall as your waist, stand one step away from them.
2. When you jump, your upper body should go straight up in the same way it did in step '6-2 backflip <Jump>'. Avoid bending or leaning your upper body backwards when you jump.
3. Just before you reach the highest point in your jump, roll your body backwards as if you were doing a somersault. Maintaining that posture, land on your back.

▶ 뒤공중 〈말기〉
▶ Backflip 〈Rolling〉

3. 자유품새의 필수기술

단계별 기술 훈련

(4) 뒤공중 〈착지〉

뒤공중 동작 후에 착지 과정으로 기술의 완성도 및 부상 예방을 위한 단계이다.

1. 매트 위에서 앉고, 손은 앞으로 들어 뒤구르기를 준비한다.

2. 뒤구르기를 진행하며 최대한 몸을 말아준다. 이때 무릎이 어깨 위를 지나간다고 생각하며 뒤구르기의 속도를 올린다.

3. 미리 몸을 피고 난 후에 착지하지 않도록 한다.

Step-by-Step Skill Training

(4) Backflip <Landing>

In this step, you will practice landing your backflip. This will help you avoid injuries and perfect your technique.

1. Sit on top of the mats with your arms outstretched in front of you, ready for a backwards somersault.

2. Do a backwards somersault with your body curled up as tightly as possible. You can increase the speed of your somersault by imagining tucking your knees so tightly into yourself that they would pass over your shoulders.

3. Straighten out your body only after landing.

▶ 측전 〈착지〉
▶ Roundoff 〈Landing〉

3.Application techniques of Freestyle Poomsae

단계별 기술 훈련

(5) 뒤공중

숙련된 보조자의 도움을 받아 시연자는 이전에 연습했던 <도약>, <회전>, <착지> 단계에 맞춰 뒤공중을 한다.
1. 시선은 정면에서 착지하는 바닥으로 이어진다. 점프 시 하체를 많이 쓰고, 양팔은 위로 올리면서 점프를 한다.
2. 뒤공중 시 무릎이 어깨 위를 지나간다고 생각하며 말아준다. 또한 '6-4. 뒤공중 <착지>' 과정처럼 착지 전까지 몸을 말고 있는 자세를 유지한다.
3. 보조자는 뒤공중 진행에 방해가 되지 않도록 옆에서 보조하며, 양손으로 허리를 받친다. 시연자와 보조자의 호흡이 중요하기 때문에 서로 소통하면서 훈련을 반복한다.

Step-by-Step Skill Training

(5) Backflip

With the assistance of an experienced spotter, perform the <jump>, <rotation>, and <landing> steps as practiced earlier.
1. You should be looking straight in front of you at the beginning of your backflip. Then, your gaze should continue on to the floor as you land. When you jump, you should be using your lower body strength while raising both arms up.
2. When you are in the air, imagine tucking your knees so tightly into yourself that they would pass over your shoulders. Keep your body in this tightly curled up position until you land, just as you practiced in '6-4, backflip <landing>'.
3. Your spotter should stand off to the side, so they do not impede your movements, and use both hands to support your waist. The coordination between you and your spotter in this step is crucial, so you should continue practicing with the same spotter, and make a point of communicating back and forth with each other.

▶ 뒤공중
▶ Backflip

3. 자유품새의 필수기술

단계별 기술 훈련

(6) 측전 뒤공중

1. 측전 후 뒤공중을 시도하는 단계이다. 안전을 위하여 장비 또는 보조자의 도움이 필요하다.
2. 초보자에게는 위험한 단계이기 때문에 숙련된 보조자의 도움 및 장비를 활용하여 안전에 대한 주의가 필요하다.

Step-by-Step Skill Training

(6) Roundoff Backflip

1. In this step, you will practice doing a backflip after a roundoff. For your safety, you will need safety equipment and/or assistance from a spotter.
2. This is a dangerous step for beginners, so proceed with caution. Ask an experienced spotter for assistance and use high quality safety equipment.

▶ 측전 뒤공중
▶ Roundoff Backflip

3.Application techniques of Freestyle Poomsae

단계별 기술 훈련

(7) 측전 뒤공중 이어차기

1. 측전 뒤공중을 하며 차기를 하는 기술로 측전 뒤공중이 숙련된 상태에서 훈련을 시작한다.
2. 보조자의 도움을 받아 제자리 뒤공중을 하며 이어차기를 한다. 이때 첫발을 상향 45° 시선에서 시작한다.
3. 측전 뒤공중을 하며 이어차기를 한다. 이때 고개를 뒤로 심하게 젖히거나 점프 시 손을 밑으로 내리지 않도록 한다.

Step-by-Step Skill Training

(7) Roundoff Backflip with Multiple Kicks

1. You should only start training for the roundoff backflip with multiple kicks after mastering the roundoff backflip.
2. With the assistance of a spotter, perform a Multiple kick. At this time, this first kick should be performed at a 45° angle.
3. While doing a roundoff backflip, perform a multiple jumping kick. Make sure not to tilt your head too far back or lower your hands while jumping.

▶ 측전 이어차기
▶ Roundoff backflip with multiple kicks

3. 자유품새의 필수기술

7) 모돌개차기

모돌개차기는 '벨트', 'B-twist' 등 다양한 명칭으로 쓰인다.

기술 명칭의 한글화에 따라 회전축을 기준으로 '모'를 앞에 두고 '돌개차기'를 붙여 명명한다.

모돌기(선자)에서 한 바퀴를 비트는 동작에서 차기를 통해 태권도 기술로 재해석 되었다.

응용 기술로는 모돌아 바깥차기(B-twist illusion)등이 있고, '후려차기-모돌개차기', '모돌아 360°(B-twist)-휘돌개차기(Corkscrew kick)' 등과 같은 연결 기술로 응용이 가능하다.

7) B-twist kick

This technique goes by a variety of different names such as 'belt', 'B-twist', etc.

The Korean technical term is 'Moh-Dolgae-Chagi'. The 'Dolgae-Chagi' refers to a tornado kick, and the 'Moh' is placed at the front of the term.

The B-twist has been reinterpreted into a Taekwondo technique through the addition of a kicking motion to the twist.

Applied techniques include the B-twist-illusion kick, as well as consecutive combination kicks such as the hook kick followed by B-twist kick, B-twist followed by Corkscrew kick.

▶ 모돌개차기
▶ B-twist kick

3.Application techniques of Freestyle Poomsae

단계별 기술 훈련

(1) 모돌기

'선자'라고 하며 기술 명칭의 한글화에 따라 '모돌기'로 명명한다.

1. 준비 자세에서 한걸음 나간 후 뒤로 발을 들어준다. 이때 어깨를 닫아주고 몸을 가볍게 띄워준다.

2. 상체가 "U"모양과 같이 양 다리를 차례로 지나가도록 한다. 이때 상체를 최대한 높게 들어주고, 양 다리를 번갈아 들어준다.

3. 착지 시 상체를 세우고, 착지 후 회전이 멈추지 않도록 한다.

Step-by-Step Skill Training

(1) Butterfly

The Butterfly is often called 'Seonja' in Korean, and the Korean technical term we would like to use is 'Moh-Dohl-Ki'.

1. From your starting position, take one step forward, then raise your leg backwards. Right at that moment, close your shoulders and lightly lift your body off the ground.

2. Let your legs pass by your upper body in a 'U'-shape, one after the other. Raise your upper body as high as you can, and lift each leg alternately.

3. As you land, keep your upper body upright. As you touch back down to the ground, continue to keep your body rotating.

▶ 모돌기
▶ Butterfly

3. 자유품새의 필수기술

단계별 기술 훈련

(2) 모돌개차기 〈비틀기〉

시선을 활용하여 모돌개차기의 비틀기 연습을 하는 단계이다.

1. 무릎 이하 높이의 보조기구에 한발을 올리고 준비한다.

2. 팔의 반동과 상체를 올리는 동작을 동시에 하여 등쪽으로 회전한다.

3. 시선의 시작과 끝을 지면으로 한다.

Step-by-Step Skill Training

(2) B-twist kick 〈Twisting〉

In this step, you will practice your B-twist kick twisting by focusing on controlling where you are looking.

1. Put one foot on top of a mat that is below the height of your knee.

2. Simultaneously raise your upper body while creating a pumping motion with your arms to provide momentum. Then, spin towards your back.

3. When you start and finish these movements, you should be looking at the ground.

▶ 모돌개차기 〈비틀기〉
▶ B-twist kick 〈Twisting〉

3.Application techniques of Freestyle Poomsae

단계별 기술 훈련

(3) 모돌개차기 <모돌아 360°>

모돌기에서 바로 몸을 한 바퀴 비튼다.

1. 시선은 '7-2. 모돌개차기 <비틀기>'과 같이 시작과 끝을 지면으로 한다.
2. 비틀기 시 상체를 올려주고, 회전 방향으로 어깨를 계속 열어주며 진행한다.
3. 모돌기 시 바로 몸을 비튼다. 비틀기를 빨리 시작할수록 한바퀴에 대한 회전이 빠르게 진행되어 차기에 적합하다.
4. 모돌개차기 시 뒷발을 들어주어 모돌기의 형태를 유지한다.

Step-by-Step Skill Training

(3) B-twist kick <B-twist>

Your body will complete one full rotation directly after the Butterfly.

1. As practiced in '7-2 B-twist kick <Twisting>, you should be looking at the ground at the start and end of these movements.
2. As you twist, raise your upper body and allow your shoulders to continue opening up in the direction you are twisting.
3. Start twisting your body immediately after starting your Butterfly. The faster you start twisting, the faster you will be able to complete a whole spin, making it easier for you to kick.
4. Raising your back leg up during your B-twist kick will help you maintain your Butterfly form.

▶ 모돌개차기 <모돌아 360°>
▶ B-twist kick <B-twist>

단계별 기술 훈련

(4) 모아 돌개차기

현재 팝턴, 팝킥등 다양한 명칭으로 사용되고 있으며 기술 명칭의 한글화에 따라 '모아 돌개차기'로 명명한다.

1. 두발로 모아 뛰어 한 바퀴 비튼다. 반동을 주며 회전을 시작하고, 양팔은 몸 쪽으로 붙이며 회전력을 더해준다. 또한 도약 시 회전에 방해가 되지 않도록 발로 지면을 짧게 밟아 뛴다.

2. 차기의 표현성을 위해 보조 발의 무릎을 들어주어 돌려차기를 한다. 이때 상체가 눕지 않도록 하며, 어깨너머로 시선처리를 한다.

3. 차기 후 시선을 정면으로 유지하며 동작을 끝낸다.

Step-by-Step Skill Training

(4) Pop Tornado Kick

The Korean technical term we would like to use is 'Moa-Dolgae-Chagi'.

1. Using both feet, do Pop Tornado Kick. Slightly swing your arms backwards, then use the forward momentum of your arms to start your twisting. You can increase your torque by bringing your arms in towards your body. When you start your jump, take a quick step so you can spin easier.

2. Raise up the knee of your supporting leg when you throw your roundhouse kick for better expression of energy. As you do this, do not lean back your upper body and make sure to look over your shoulder.

3. After kicking, finish your movements by fixing your gaze straight ahead.

▶ 모아 돌개차기
▶ Pop Torando Kick

3.Application techniques of Freestyle Poomsae

단계별 기술 훈련

(5) 모돌개차기

'7-3. 모돌개차기 <모돌아 360°>' 과정과 '7-4. 모아 돌개차기' 과정을 동시에 시도한다.

1. '7-3.모돌개차기 <모돌아 360°> ' 과정에서 시선만 차는 곳으로 옮겨주어 돌려차기를 한다.
2. 비틀기를 빨리 시작할수록 한바퀴에 대한 회전이 빠르게 진행되어 차기에 적합하다.

Step-by-Step Skill Training

(5) B-twist kick

Here, you will simultaneously attempt steps '7-3 B-twist' and '7-4 Pop Tornado Kick'.

1. While doing step '7-3 B-twist', move your gaze towards your kicking target and throw a roundhouse kick.
2. The faster you start twisting, the faster you will be able to complete a whole rotation, making it easier for you to kick.

▶ 모돌개차기
▶ B-twist kick

3. 자유품새의 필수기술

8) 휘돌개차기

휘돌개차기는 '하우스벨트', 'Corkscrew' 등 다양한 명칭으로 쓰인다.

기술 명칭의 한글화에 따라 '마구 돈다'라는 뜻을 가진 '휘돌다'의 '휘'를 앞에 두고 '돌개차기'를 붙여 '휘돌개차기'로 명명한다.

휘돌기(하우스턴)에서 한 바퀴를 회전하는 동작에서 차기를 통해 태권도 기술로 재해석 되었다.

응용 기술로는 휘돌아 바깥차기 등이 있고, '안짚기-휘돌개차기', '돌개차기-휘돌개차기' 처럼 연결 기술로 응용이 가능하다

8) Corkscrew kick

This technique has many different terms, such as 'Corkscrew', 'housebelt', etc.

The Korean technical term is 'Hwi-Dolgae-Chagi', which carries the meaning, 'to turn around'. The 'Hwi' is put at the beginning of the word, and combined with 'Dolgae-Chagi' to create the word, 'Hwi-Dolgae-Chagi'.

The gainer has been reinterpreted into a Taekwondo technique through the addition of a kick after the completion of a single rotation.

Applied techniques include the Corkscrew illusion kick, among others. They can also include combination techniques such as scoot-Corkscrew kick, 'tornado kick Corkscrew kick.

▶ 휘돌개차기
▶ Corkscrew Kick

3.Application techniques of Freestyle Poomsae

단계별 기술 훈련

(1) 휘돌개차기 〈회전〉

'하우스턴'이라고 하며 기술 명칭의 한글화에 따라 '휘돌기'로 명명한다.

1. 상체는 비틀고, 손은 교차하여 가슴으로 모아주며 한걸음 나간다.
2. 한걸음 나간 후에 양팔과 뒤에 있던 발을 동시에 사선으로 올리며 회전을 시작한다.
3. 올렸던 발을 균형있게 사용하여 착지 시 상체를 세운다.

Step-by-Step Skill Training

(1) Corkscrew kick <Rotation>

The Korean terminology for cheat gainer is 'Hwi-Dolgi'.

1. Twist your upper body, then cross your hands and draw them towards your chest while you take one step forward.
2. After taking one step forward, raise your back leg and both arms up diagonally, starting your rotation.
3. Use your raised foot to stabilize your balance, and straighten your upper body as you land.

▶ 휘돌개차기 〈회전〉
▶ Corkscrew Kick 〈Rotation〉

3. 자유품새의 필수기술

단계별 기술 훈련

(2) 휘돌개차기 <동선>

휘돌기를 위한 동선을 만들어주는 단계이다.

1. '8-1. 휘돌개차기 <회전>'에서 양손을 같이 착지하여 몸을 숙인다.

2. 발을 디딜 때 몸의 중심을 막아주듯이 사용하고, 제자리에서 동작을 실행한다.

3. 올바른 동선을 만들기 위해 양팔과 다리를 함께 사용한다.

Step-by-Step Skill Training

(2) Corkscrew kick <Moving line>

In this step, you will practice creating the appropriate swinging line of motion for your Corkscrew.

1. Do step '8-1 Corkscrew <Rotation>', but plant both hands on the ground and bend your upper body over.

2. When taking one step forward, imagine stopping your body's centre of gravity from being shifted forward, finishing the rest of your movements in place.

3. Use your arms and legs to form the proper movement trajectory.

▶ 휘돌개차기 <동선>
▶ Corkscrew Kick <Moving line>

3.Application techniques of Freestyle Poomsae

단계별 기술 훈련

(3) 휘돌개차기 〈휘돌기〉

'하우스턴' 또는 'Cheat Gainer' 라고 하며 기술 명칭의 한글화에 따라 '휘돌기'로 명명한다

1. '8-2. 휘돌개차기 <동선>에서 착지 시 사용했던 양손을 사용하지 않고 발로만 착지한다.
2. 도약 시 착지 지점을 바라보며 상체를 숙여주어 올바른 휘돌기의 모양을 만든다.
3. 착지 시 두 발이 지면에 닿을 때까지 회전이 진행되어야 한다.

Step-by-Step Skill Training

(3) Corkscrew kick <Cheat Gainer>

This step is called the 'Houseturn' or 'Cheat Gainer'. The Korean technical term is called "Hwi-Dolgui".

1. Do step '8-2 Corkscrew <Moving line>', but instead of using both hands to land, use only your feet.
2. For the correct form for a cheat gainer, look at your landing point when you take off, and bend your upper body.
3. The rotation shall proceed until both feet touch the ground.

▶ 휘돌개차기 〈휘돌기〉
▶ Corkscrew Kick 〈Cheat Gainer〉

3. 자유품새의 필수기술

단계별 기술 훈련

(4) 휘돌개차기 <휘돌아 360°>

'하우스벨트', 'Corkscrew' 로 불리 우는 동작이고, 휘돌기에서 바로 몸을 한 바퀴 비튼다.

1. 시선은 '8-3. 휘돌개차기 <휘돌기>' 와 같이 시작과 끝을 지면으로 한다.
2. 비틀기 시 상체를 숙여주고, 회전 방향으로 어깨를 계속 열어주며 진행한다.
3. 휘돌기 시 바로 몸을 회전한다. 비틀기를 빨리 시작할수록 한바퀴에 대한 회전이 빠르게 진행되어 차기에 적합하다.
4. 휘돌아 360° 시 앞발을 들어주고 상체를 숙이며 휘돌기의 형태를 유지한다.

Step-by-Step Skill Training

(4) Corkscrew kick <Corkscrew>

This is a technique that is called 'housebelt' or 'Corkscrew'. From a cheat gainer, turn your body one additional twist.

1. At the start and end of your movements, your gaze should be affixed in the same manner as it is in step '8-3 Cheat Gainer'.
2. While you twist, lower your upper body and open up your shoulders in the direction you are turning.
3. Immediately continue to spin your body after the cheat gainer. The faster you start to twist, the faster you will complete the rotation for your first turn, making it easier to kick.
4. To maintain the proper form for a Corkscrew, raise up your front leg and lower your upper body during your Cheat Gainer.

▶ 휘돌아 360°
▶ Corkscrew Kick <Corkscrew>

3.Application techniques of Freestyle Poomsae

단계별 기술 훈련

(5) 휘돌개차기

'8-4. 휘돌개차기 <휘돌아 360°>' 과정과 '7-4. 모아 돌개차기' 과정을 동시에 시도한다.

1. '8-4. 휘돌개차기 <휘돌아 360°>' 과정에서 시선만 차는 곳으로 옮겨주어 돌려차기를 한다.
2. 회전을 빨리 시작할수록 한바퀴에 대한 회전이 빠르게 진행되어 차기에 적합하다.

Step-by-Step Skill Training

(5) Corkscrew kick

In this step, you will simultaneously do steps '8-4 Corkscrew ' and '7-4. Pop Tornado Kick'.

1. Do step '8-4. Corkscrew ', but instead of looking where you plan to land, look where you are planning to kick, then throw a roundhouse kick.
2. The faster you start to spin, the faster you will complete the spin for your first turn, making it easier to kick.

▶ 휘돌개차기
▶ Corkscrew Kick

3. 자유품새의 필수기술

9) 옆돌아 돌개차기

옆돌아 돌개차기는 '팝턴', '훌턴' 등 다양한 명칭으로 쓰인다.

기술 명칭의 한글화에 따라 도움 받는 형태를 기준으로 '옆돌아'를 앞에 두고 '돌개차기'를 붙여 명명한다.

손을 옆으로 짚는 도움닫기 후 모아 돌개차기를 하며 태권도 기술로 재해석 되었다.

파생 기술로는 '옆돌아 540° 후려차기', '옆돌아 연속 후려차기' 등이 있고, '후려차기-옆돌아 돌개차기' 처럼 연결기술로 응용이 가능하다.

9) Cartwheel full twist kick

Cartwheel full twist kick is called by various other names, such as 'pop-turn' or 'full-turn'.

The Korean terminology, is named after the the 'Yeop-Dola' (cartwheel) motion that precedes the 'Dolgae-Chagi' (tornado kick).

This kick has been adopted as a Taekwondo technique through the integration of hands pushing off the ground on either side, then Pop Tornado Kick.

Related techniques include 'Hyper hook kick,' 'Shurikken hyper hook kick' etc.

This kick can be used as a combination technique such as 'hook kick-Cartwheel full twist kick'.

▶ 옆돌아 돌개차기
▶ Cartwheel full twist kick

3.Application techniques of Freestyle Poomsae

단계별 기술 훈련

(1) 옆돌기

옆으로 손을 짚고 다리를 넘기며 도움닫기를 하는 과정이다.

1. 어깨를 닫으며 반동과 함께 상체를 허벅지에 붙이며 기술을 진행한다.
2. 옆돌기 시 다리를 빠르게 넘겨 도약력을 높인다.
3. 몸이 살짝 앞을 향하는 자세로 끝낸다.

Step-by-Step Skill Training

(1) Cartwheel

Planting both hands on the ground to one side, raise your legs into the air.

1. Close your shoulders and put your upper body against your thighs upon recoil.
2. Increase air time by focusing on moving your legs quickly.
3. Your body should be leaning slightly forwards upon completion of this technique.

▶ 옆돌기
▶ Cartwheel

3. 자유품새의 필수기술

단계별 기술 훈련

(2) 짚고 후려차기 후 모아 돌개차기

옆돌아 돌개차기를 위한 중간과정을 연습하는 방법이다.

1. 손으로 지면을 짚으며 후려차기를 한다. 후려차기 시 동시에 손을 짚도록 한다.

2. 후려차기 시 어깨를 닫아주고, 차기 후 동시에 상체를 세우면서 동작을 끝낸다.

3. 후려차기 후 발이 땅에 닿자마자 모아 돌개차기를 찬다. 이때 정면을 주시하여 회전한다

Step-by-Step Skill Training

(2) Touch Hook Kick followed by a Pop Tornado Kick

In this step, you will practice progression for cartwheel full twist kick.

1. Touch the ground with your hand at the same time you kick out on the hook kick.

2. Make sure to close the shoulders when kicking. Finish the motion by standing your torso up immediately following the kick.

3. As soon as your feet touch the ground after the hook kick, follow it up with a pop tornado kick. Look straight ahead as you turn.

▶ 짚고 후려차기 후 모아 돌개차기
▶ Touch Hook Kick followed by a Pop Tornado Kick

3.Application techniques of Freestyle Poomsae

단계별 기술 훈련

(3) 옆돌아 돌개차기

1. '9-2. 짚고 후려차기 후 모아 돌개차기' 와 같이 옆돌기에서 발이 지면에 닿자마자 뛰며 옆돌기의 가속을 받아 도약한다.
2. 옆돌기 후 정면을 주시한 후 모아 돌개차기를 찬다.
3. 옆돌기 시 팔을 적절히 사용하여 상체를 빠르게 들어주고, 옆돌기 후 도약할 때 몸을 열어주면서 비틀기를 시작한다.

Step-by-Step Skill Training

(3) Cartwheel full twist kick

1. As soon as your feet touch the ground after cartwheel, use your momentum to jump off the ground.
2. After the cartwheel, look straight ahead. Then, do a pop tornado kick.
3. During the cartwheel, use your arms to quickly lift your torso up. After the cartwheel, open up your body as you jump and start the twisting.

▶ 옆돌아 돌개차기
▶ Cartwheel full twist kick

3. 자유품새의 필수기술

10) 짚기

짚기는 손을 땅에 짚는 동작을 말하며, 크게 두가지로 나눌 수 있다.

몸 안쪽으로 돌며 짚는 기술인 'Scoot'과 몸 바깥쪽으로 돌며 짚는 'Touch Down Rise'가 있다.

기술 명칭의 한글화에 따라 이하 몸이 움직이는 형태를 기준으로 'Scoot'은 '안짚기','Touch Down Rise'는 '바깥짚기'로 명명한다.

짚기는 측전, 옆돌기처럼 본동작에서 힘을 받기 위해 시도하는 도움닫기라고 할 수 있다.

연결 기술로는 휘돌기, 휘돌개차기, 휘돌아 540°후려차기 등이 있다.

10) Scoot and Touch Down Rise

The 'Jipki' refers to the motion of planting your hand on the ground, and it can be divided into two types of motions.

Planting your hand while turning inwards is called a 'Scoot', and planting your hand while turning your body outwards is called a 'Touch Down Rise'.

The Korean technical terms, is 'An-Jipki' for 'Scoot', and 'Baggat-Jipki' for 'Touch Down Rise'.

Just like the roundoff and side-turn, the scoot and touch down rise are supporting techniques that help gather the momentum and power needed for the main technique.

Connecting techniques include the cheat gainer, corkscrew kick, box cutter spinning hook kick, etc.

▶ 짚기
▶ Scoot and Touch Down Rise

3.Application techniques of Freestyle Poomsae

단계별 기술 훈련

(1) 안짚기

몸 안쪽으로 돌며 지면을 짚고 몸을 이동하는 도움닫기이다.

1. 한쪽 무릎을 세우고 몸의 방향은 대각선으로 앉는다.
2. 시선은 정면을 주시하고, 옆돌기처럼 팔을 흔들어 반동을 준다.
3. 회전 방향에 맞추어 손을 열어주며 지면을 짚는다.
4. 손을 짚는 동시에 무릎을 떼며 동작을 시작하고, 안짚기 시 몸을 틀어 진행한다.

Step-by-Step Skill Training

(1) Scoot

This is a supporting technique where you turn towards the inside of your body and plant your hand on the ground.

1. Sit with one knee straightened out and your body facing diagonally.
2. You should be looking straight ahead. Swing your arms to the side across your body as if you are doing a cartwheel to get momentum.
3. Depending on the direction you are spinning, open up the appropriate hand, planting your palm on the ground.
4. Start by lifting your knee at the very moment your hand touches the ground, and turn your body as you do your scoot.

▶ 안짚기
▶ Scoot

3. 자유품새의 필수기술

단계별 기술 훈련

(2) 안짚기 – 휘돌기 〈연결〉

1. 안짚기 후 양팔과 다리를 동시에 올리며 바로 '8-1 휘돌개차기 〈회전〉'을 한다.

2. 회전 시 안정적인 진행을 위해 올렸던 다리를 빠르게 내려놓는다.

Step-by-Step Skill Training

(2) Scoot – Cheat Gainer <Connection>

1. After doing a scoot, raise both your arms and your leg upwards and go straight into step '8-1 Corkscrew <Rotation>'.

2. To stabilize your spin, quickly lower the leg you previously raised upwards.

▶ 안짚기 – 휘돌개차기 〈연결〉
▶ Scoot – Cheat Gainer 〈Connection〉

3.Application techniques of Freestyle Poomsae

단계별 기술 훈련

(3) 안짚기 – 휘돌기

1. '10-2 안짚기-휘돌기 <연결>' 이 완성되면, 안짚기 후 휘돌기를 한다.
2. 안짚기 후 시선은 착지할 곳을 향하고, 동시에 다리를 차올리며 휘돌기를 한다.

Step-by-Step Skill Training

(3) Scoot – Cheat Gainer

1. When step '10-2 Scoot – Cheat Gainer <Connection>' is successfully completed, add a cheat gainer after the scoot.
2. After the scoot, look at where you will land and simultaneously kick up your legs into a cheat gainer.

▶ 안짚기-휘돌기
▶ Scoot – Cheat Gainer

3. 자유품새의 필수기술

단계별 기술 훈련

(4) 바깥짚기 〈회전〉

1. 동작을 쉽게 접근하기 위해 돌개차기의 형태에서 변형하여 기술을 이해한다.
2. 어깨를 닫았다가 열어주며 회전 반동을 주고, 옆으로 이동하며 기술을 진행한다.
3. 디딛는 발을 짧게 찍어 밟는 동시에 반대 발과 양팔을 들어주며 회전을 계속 진행한다.
4. 차기는 하지 않고 보조발을 돌리며 회전만 진행한다. 착지 시 시선은 지면을 향하고, 몸의 방향이 뒤돌아 끝날 수 있도록 한다.

Step-by-Step Skill Training

(4) Touch Down Rise <Spin>

1. An easy way of understanding how to do this technique is by modifying the tornado kick.
2. For momentum, slightly wind up your body then spring it forwards by closing your shoulders then opening them up. This technique is done laterally.
3. A short stomping motion should be made by the foot taking a step, and at the same time, the opposite foot and both arms should be lifted up to continue spinning.
4. Instead of being used to kick, turn the foot of the supporting leg in order to spin. When landing, look at the ground and make your body face backwards as you finish your movements.

▶ 바깥짚기 〈회전〉
▶ Touch Down Rise 〈Spin〉

3.Application techniques of Freestyle Poomsae

단계별 기술 훈련

(5) 바깥짚기 〈동선〉

1. '10-4. 바깥짚기 〈회전〉' 이 완성되면, 손을 짚어 바깥짚기의 동선을 만들어 준다.

2. 시작 시 발을 교차하며 들어주고, 착지 발과 같은 방향의 손을 동시에 지면에 짚는다.

3. 짚는 손의 방향은 살짝 닫아주고 팔은 귀에 최대한 붙인다.

Step-by-Step Skill Training

(5) Touch Down Rise <Moving line>

1. After successfully completing '10-4 Touch Down Rise <Spin>', create the appropriate movement trajectory for the touch down rise by planting your hand on the ground.

2. When you start, lift your legs one at a time, and simultaneously plant the hand that is on the side of your landing foot on the ground.

3. Slightly close your body off from the side your planted hand is on and stick your arm as close to your ear as possible.

▶ 바깥짚기 〈동선〉
▶ Touch Down Rise 〈Moving line〉

단계별 기술 훈련

(6) 바깥짚기

몸 바깥쪽으로 돌며 지면을 짚고 몸을 이동하는 도움닫기이다.

1. '10-5. 바깥짚기 <동선>' 이 완성되면 과감하게 바깥짚기를 시도한다.

2. 바깥짚기 시 어깨를 닫으며 반동과 함께 양팔을 동시에 돌리며 시작한다.

3. 발을 교차하며 보조발을 높게 올려주고, 짚는 손에 적절히 체중이 실려야 한다.

Step-by-Step Skill Training

(6) Touch Down Rise

Pushing off the ground with one hand, while rotating towards the outside of the body, this is a technique that helps to prepare and provide more momentum for following techniques.

1. After successfully completing step '10-5 Touch Down Rise <Moving line>' boldly attempt the touch down rise.

2. During the touch down rise, close your shoulders and start the technique by rotating both arms with a slight bouncing motion for momentum.

3. Lift your feet one at a time, raise your supporting foot high while transferring your weight to your hand.

▶ 바깥짚기
▶ Touch Down Rise

3.Application techniques of Freestyle Poomsae

11) 기술 강화 훈련
(1) 점프 런지 스쿼트

뛰어 옆차기를 완성도있게 수행하기 위해서는 체공능력이 중요하다. 공중으로 순발력있게 솟구쳐 올라가는 훈련을 통해 안정된 체공 시간을 확보할 수 있다.

1. 앞굽이의 형태에서 무릎을 끌어 올리며 최대한 높고 빠르게 도약 자세를 만들어 준다.

2. 도약 자세를 만든 후 가능한 만큼 자세를 유지하여 공중에서의 신체 균형 능력을 향상 시킬 수 있다

11) Skill-Enhancement Training
(1) Jump Lunge Squat

Increasing airtime during jumping side kick is key to perfecting your jumping side kick. By enhancing your ability to agilely leap into the air, you can increase your airtime. In turn, this will increase the stability of your midair kicking position.

It is important increase airtime in order to perform better jumping side kick. Increased airtime can be produced by practicing various explosive jumping excercises.

1. Start in a kneeling position similar to a forward stance. Then, assume your jumping position by raising your knee as high and as quickly as possible.

2. After moving into the jumping position, hold the position as long as you can to improve your balance in the air.

▶ 점프 런지 스쿼트
▶ Jump Lunge Squat

3. 자유품새의 필수기술

(2) 도약 후 다리 모으기

1. 도움닫기로 세걸음 도약 후 몸을 최대한 모아준다.

2. 최대한 빨리 다리를 끌어 모으며, 가능한 오래 유지한 후에 착지한다.

(2) Gathering the Legs Together After Jumping

1. Lead into your jump by taking three steps forward. After your jump, gather your body together as closely as possible.

2. Gather your legs towards your body as quickly as you can, holding this position for as long as possible before landing.

▶ 도약 후 다리 모으기
▶ Gathering the Legs Together After Jumping

3. Application techniques of Freestyle Poomsae

(3) 보조기구 뛰어 넘기

1. 세 걸음 도움닫기를 통해 보조기구를 뛰어 넘는다.

2. 도움닫기 속도를 점점 빠르게 하며, 도약 후 공중에서 보조발을 한 번 더 끌어당기며 보조기구를 넘는다.

(3) Jumping Over Training Equipment

1. Take three steps leading into a jump over some training equipment.

2. Gradually increase the speed of the your steps. After taking off for your jump over the training equipment, pull your supporting leg up towards your body.

▶ 보조기구 뛰어 넘기
▶ Jumping Over Training Equipment

3. 자유품새의 필수기술

(4) 제자리 도약 차기

1. 첫번째 발을 끌어 올리는 감각을 훈련하는 단계이다. 시연자는 첫번째 타겟과 한 걸음 정도의 위치에서 도약한다. 양 팔을 힘차게 흔들며 앞차기 3단계를 시도하고, 첫번째 타겟을 차면서 동시에 도약 한다.

2. 첫번째 타겟을 찬 후 두번째, 세번째 차기는 무릎만 교차하고 착지한다.

3. 공중에서 교차로 무릎올리기가 익숙해지면 차기를 연속해서 찬다.

(4) Stationary Jump Kicking

This step helps you get a feel for how to raise your foot for your first kick. Jump into the air when you are about one step away from the first target. You should kick the first target as you start your jump. Try to do jumping triple front kicks while forcefully pumping your arms back and forth for momentum (as in a running motion).

Kick the first target, but replace your second and third kicks with alternating knee-ups before landing.

Once you become used to the feeling of switching knees in the air, replace the knee raises with consecutive front kicks.

▶ 제자리 도약 차기
▶ Stationary Jump Kicking

3. Application techniques of Freestyle Poomsae

(5) 속도 차기

1. 2인 1조로 마주보고 위치한다. 시연자는 차기 준비 자세를 취하고, 보조자는 앉아서 무릎 높이로 타겟을 잡아준다.

2. 양 발을 최대한 빠르게 교차하며 연속해서 앞차기를 찬다. 이때 상체는 세우고 팔은 힘차게 위아래로 빠르게 번갈아 들어올린다. 특히 차는 순간 발목을 편다.

(5) Speed Kicking

1. This step must be practiced with a partner. Have your partner sit on the ground and hold a target at knee-level. You should be facing your partner, ready to kick.

2. Alternating legs with each front kick, throw a consecutive series of kicks. Switch your legs and bring up your knees as quickly as possible. Your body should be upright and you should be forcefully pumping your arms back and forth for momentum (as in a running motion). Straighten out your ankle only as you kick.

▶ 속도 차기
▶ Speed kicking

3. 자유품새의 필수기술

(6) 공중 연속차기

1. 두 팔로 보조기구를 지탱하고 한발 도약을 하여 차기를 한다.

2. 보조기구를 통해 체공 시간을 늘려 앞차기를 연속하여 최대한 많이 차고 착지한다.

3. 차기의 높이는 허리 위로 차도록 한다.

(6) Consecutive Kicks in Midair

1. Standing between two objects you can use for support on either side, use your arms for support as you jump off the ground with one leg and kick.

2. Use the supporting objects to extend your air time and perform as many consecutive kicks as possible before landing.

3. Make sure you are kicking over your waist.

▶ 공중 연속차기
▶ Consecutive Kicks in Midair

3.Application techniques of Freestyle Poomsae

(7) 연속발차기 〈딛기〉

다양한 딛기를 연속하여 수행 시, 겨룸새와 보폭을 유지하며 시선은 정면을 주시한다.

1. 제자리 전·후 딛기 : 내딛기, 물러 딛기와 다르게 두발이 지면에서 동시에 떨어져 전·후로 움직인다.

2. 제자리 전·후 딛기를 2회 연속 반복한다.

3. 내딛기 : 앞에 있는 발이 먼저 앞쪽으로 내딛으며 나가고 뒷발이 지면을 밀어주며 앞으로 이동한다.

4. 내딛기를 2회 연속 반복한다.

(7) Kyorugi Style Consecutive Kicking <Footwork>

When executing various footwork combinations, maintain your sparring stance and stride length while fixing your gaze forward.

1. Stepping in place forwards and backwards: Unlike a forward step or a backward step, both feet simultaneously lift off the ground and move forwards or backwards together.

2. Repeat step one twice in quick succession.

3. Forward step: The front foot steps forward first, followed by the back foot which pushes off the ground and slides forward.

4. Repeat a forward step two times consecutively.

▶ 연속발차기 〈딛기〉
▶ Kyorugi Style Consecutive Kicking 〈Footwork〉

3. 자유품새의 필수기술

5. 물러딛기 : 내딛기와 반대로 뒷발이 먼저 뒤쪽으로 물러준 후 앞발이 지면을 밀어주며 뒤로 이동한다.
6. 물러딛기를 2회 연속 반복한다.
7. 발붙여 내딛기 : 뒷발이 앞발을 쳐주듯이 앞으로 이동할 때, 앞발도 함께 앞으로 이동한다.
8. 모딛기 : 앞발을 가볍게 앞으로 눌러주며 뒷발을 옆으로 옮겨준 후 앞발은 진행방향으로 이동한다.
9. 옆딛기 : 앞발을 축으로 등 쪽으로 회전하며 앞으로 이동한다.
10. 오른 돌아딛기 : 왼발을 중심으로 오른발을 90° 뒤로 이동한다.
11. 돌아딛기 : 앞발을 중심으로 뒷발을 180° 뒤로 이동한다.

5. Backward step: Opposite of a forward step, the back foot first takes a step backwards, then the front foot pushes off the ground to take a sliding step backwards.
6. Repeat a backward step two times consecutively.
7. Skipping forward step: The back foot is brought towards the front foot, almost as if it were hitting the front foot. The front foot moves forwards as the back foot does.
8. Diagonal step: Using the front foot to lightly push down on the ground, the back foot is moved to the side. Then, the front foot is moved in the direction the back foot has moved.
9. Side step: Keep your front foot stationary and move your back foot to the side.
10. Right turning step: Keeping your left leg in place, turn your right foot backwards 90°.
11. Turning step: Keeping your front leg in place, move the back leg backwards 180°.

▶ 연속발차기 〈딛기〉
▶ Kyorugi Style Consecutive Kicking 〈Footwork〉

3. Application techniques of Freestyle Poomsae

(8) 무릎 올리기

연속차기 시 전진하며 연결해야 하는 동작에서 축이 되는 발의 이동이 원활하여야 공격력 있는 차기를 표현할 수 있다.

1. 무릎을 올리는 발을 지면에 닿지 않도록 하여 전진하며, 연속으로 무릎을 올려준다. 상체를 곧게 유지하고 엉덩이가 빠지지않도록 주의한다.

2. 지면에 발을 닿도록 하여 양발을 번갈아 짧게 나가며 무릎을 올려준다. 축이 되는 발 진행 방향으로 이동해야 한다.

(8) Knee Ups

For consecutive kicks, an attacking kick can only be properly expressed when your kicking foot moves smoothly, your movements are connected, and your body continues moving forward.

1. Move forwards without letting the foot of the raised knee touch the ground, then raise your knees consecutively. Keep your upper body straight and make sure your hips do not drop down.

2. Without jumping off of the ground, alternate raising your knees up while taking short steps forward. You should be moving in the direction your supporting leg is facing.

▶ 무릎 올리기
▶ Knee Ups

3. 자유품새의 필수기술

3. 뒷발이 한걸음 빠르게 내디뎌 전진하여 무릎을 올려준다.

4. 나래차기 형태로 무릎올리며 뒷발을 사선으로 올려 약 70%의 힘을 준 뒤 두 번째 동작의 무릎을 100%의 힘으로 올려준다. 첫 동작보다 두 번째 동작의 힘을 더 넣어주는 것이 중요하다.

5. 4의 동작과 같은 방법으로 진행하고, 세 번을 연속하여 무릎을 올려준다. 무릎의 높이는 하, 중, 상의 순서로 올려준다.

3. Take a quick step forward with your back leg, then do a knee-up with your front leg.

4. Raise your knee as if you were doing a double kick. The first knee up with your back leg should be raised diagonally with 70% power, while the second knee up should be given 100% power. It is important to put more power into the second knee-up than the first one.

5. Repeat the previous step consecutively, with the first set of knee-ups aimed towards your low section, the second set towards your middle section, and the last set towards your high section.

▶ 무릎 올리기
▶ Knee Ups 2

3. Application techniques of Freestyle Poomsae

(9) 뒤공중 〈두발차기〉

뒤공중을 하며 두발 앞차기를 하는 기술이다.

1. 제자리 점프 후에 두발 앞차기를 훈련 한다.

2. 다리는 적당한 넓이로 벌려 차고, 뒤공중의 최고점에서 차도록 한다.

3. 시선은 항상 발을 주시하고, 허벅지 뒤쪽을 양손으로 잡아주며 회전에 안정감을 더해준다.

(9) Backflip <straddle kick>

This is a technique where a straddle kick is demonstrated during a backflip.

1. Practice doing a straddle kick after jumping up on the spot

2. Kick with your legs at a reasonable width apart. You should be kicking at the highest point of your back flip.

3. Always keep your eyes on your feet, and hold the back of your thighs with both hands. This will increase the stability of the rotation.

▶ 뒤공중 〈두발차기〉
▶ Backflip 〈straddle kick〉

3. 자유품새의 필수기술

(10) 뒤공중 〈이어차기〉

뒤공중을 하며 앞차기를 여러 번 차는 기술이다.

1. 처음에는 한 번만 차고, 점진적으로 차는 횟수를 더한다.

2. 보조자의 도움을 받아 체공시간을 확보하여 차기의 정확성을 높인다.

3. 2-3의 '뛰어 앞차기 〈연속 차기〉' 과정을 통해 여러번 차는 훈련을 한다.

(10) Backflip <Multiple Kick>

This is a technique where multiple front kicks are executed during a backflip.

1. Begin with one kick, then gradually increase the number of kicks.

2. Increase your airtime with the assistance of a helper, so you can work on increasing the accuracy of your kicks.

3. Practice multiple consecutive kicks by following the steps in '2-3 Jumping Front Kick <Consecutive Kicks>'.

▶ 뒤공중 〈이어차기〉
▶ Backflip 〈Multiple Kick〉

3. Application techniques of Freestyle Poomsae

(11) 뒤공중 〈뒤후려차기〉

뒤공중을 하며 뒤후려차는 기술이다. 뒤공중을 하며 상체를 옆으로 틀어 후려차기를 한다.

몸을 비트는 동시에 양손으로 차는 다리를 잠시 잡았다가 놓으면서 후려차기를 한다.

1. 뒤공중의 점프를 시작하며 상체를 허벅지에 붙인다고 생각하고 후려차는 다리를 가슴 쪽으로 올린다. 동시에 몸을 비틀어 뒤공중 후려차기의 동작을 만든다.

2. 뒤공중의 짧은 체공시간 내에 회전과 차기가 동시에 이루어지기 때문에 뒤공중이 매우 익숙한 상태에서 시도한다.

(11) Backflip <T-Grab Hook Kick>

This is a technique where a hook kick is demonstrated during a backflip. Turn your upper body sideways during your backflip, then do a hook kick.

1. As you start your jump for the backflip, think about gluing your thighs to your upper body and raising the knee of your kicking leg towards your chest. Simultaneously turn your body to the side while preparing the chamber for a hook kick.

2. This technique should only be attempted after you are very comfortable with backflips, as you need to both rotate and kick simultaneously in the very short window of time that you are in the air.

▶ 뒤공중 후려차기
▶ Backflip
  〈T-Grab Hook Kick〉

3. 자유품새의 필수기술

12) 기술차기의 응용

(1) 모돌아 바깥차기

'B-twist Illusion'이라고 하며 기술 명칭의 한글화에 따라 '모돌아 바깥차기'로 명명한다. 모돌개차기에서 도약했던 발로 바깥차기를 찬다.

1. '7-5. 모돌개차기'과정에서 시선만 차는 곳으로 옮겨주어 바깥차기를 한다.

2. 높은 완성도를 위해 골반을 활용하여 발을 높게 찬다.

12) Variation of Kicks

(1) B-twist Illusion Kick

We would like to introduce 'Moh-Dolgae-Chagi' as a Korean terminology for B-twist Illusion. The kick in the twisting kick should be thrown by the leg used to jump in the B-twist.

1. While doing step '7-5 B-twist kick', look at your kicking target and throw a twisting kick.

2. To perfect this technique, use your hips as you would in a twisting kick and make sure to kick high.

▶ 모돌아 바깥차기
▶ B-twist Illusion Kick

3. Application techniques of Freestyle Poomsae

(2) 뒤후려차기 -> 모돌개차기

모돌개차기를 하기 전에 다른 기술과 연결하여 난이도를 올릴 수 있다.

1. 뒤후려차기 후 모돌기에 필요한 상체의 반동을 주어 모돌개차기를 수행한다.

2. 뒤후려차기 시 어깨를 닫아 주어 상체의 반동을 이용한다.

3. 안정적인 연결을 위해 시선을 정면으로 유지한다.

(2) Hook Kick -> B-twist Kick

You can add other connecting techniques before the B-twist kick to increase the level of difficulty of the technique.

1. After throwing a hook kick, swing your arms slightly backwards, then use the forward motion of your arms for the momentum necessary for the B-twist.

2. During your hook kick, close off your shoulders and create a counter-rotation motion that goes against the momentum of your kick.

3. Keep your gaze fixed straight ahead for stable footing for the next connecting technique.

▶ 뒤후려차기 -> 모돌개차기
▶ Hook kick -> B-twist kick

3. 자유품새의 필수기술

(3) 모돌아 360° –〉 휘돌개차기

모돌아 360° 착지 후 다른 기술과 연결하여 난이도를 올릴 수 있다.

1. 모돌아 360° 착지 후 찬 발을 지면에 닿지 않고 바로 차올리며 휘돌개차기를 한다.

2. 모돌아 360° 착지 시 상체를 완벽히 세워야 안정적으로 휘돌개차기를 할 수 있다.

3. 모돌아 360° 에서 휘돌개차기로 연결 시 양팔은 다리와 함께 올린 후 몸 쪽으로 모아준다.

(3) B-Twist – Corkscrew kick

You can add other connecting techniques after the B-twist to increase the difficulty level of your techniques.

1. After landing your B-twist, immediately swing the leg that kicked into a Corkscrew, without letting it touch the ground.

2. When landing the B-twist, keeping your body completely vertical will give you a stable Corkscrew.

3. When connecting a B-twist with a Corkscrew kick, first, raise up your arms and legs, then gather them inwards towards your body.

▶ 모돌아 360° –〉 휘돌개차기
▶ B-twist –〉 Corkscrew Kick

3. Application techniques of Freestyle Poomsae

(4) 휘돌아 바깥차기

'Corkscrew Illusion' 이라고 하며 기술 명칭의 한글화에 따라 '휘돌아 바깥차기'로 명명한다. 휘돌개차기에서 도약했던 발로 바깥차기를 한다.

1. '8-5. 휘돌개차기' 과정에서 시선만 차는 곳으로 옮겨주어 바깥차기를 한다.

2. 높은 완성도를 위해 골반을 활용하여 발을 높게 찬다.

(4) Corkscrew Illusion Kick

This technique is called the 'Corkscrew Illusion', and the Korean technical term is 'Hwi-Do-la-Bagatchagi'. The twisting kick is thrown using the foot that was used to jump up in the Corkscrew.

1. Do step '8-5. Corkscrew Kick', but look at where you are aiming to kick, then throw a twisting kick.

2. To perfect this technique, kick high, and use your hips when throwing your twisting kick.

▶ 휘돌아 바깥차기
▶ Corkscrew Illusion Kick

3. 자유품새의 필수기술

(5) 안짚기 - 휘돌개차기

특수 기술 중 안짚기 또는 바깥짚기와 휘돌개차기를 연결하여 난이도를 올릴 수 있다.

1. 안짚기 후 한발을 지면에 닿지않고 바로 차올리며 연결하여 휘돌개차기를 한다.

2. 안짚기 후 휘돌개차기의 회전을 위하여 시선은 지면을 향하고 힘차게 다리를 올려 휘돌개차기를 한다.

3. 안정적인 착지를 위하여 비틀기 시 도약하는 발의 골반이 위쪽으로 올라가며 진행한다

(5) Scoot - Corkscrew Kick

You can raise the difficulty of the required techniques by connecting Touch Down Rise or Scoot to a Corkscrew.

1. After a Scoot, raise one foot up immediately so it leads into a Corkscrew without touching the ground.

2. After the Scoot, you should be looking at the ground. Powerfully lift up your legs into a Corkscrew rotation.

3. For a stable landing, raise up the hip of the leg you used to jump into your spin while twisting.

▶ 안짚기 - 휘돌개차기
▶ Scoot- Corkscrew kick

3.Application techniques of Freestyle Poomsae

(6) 돌개차기 – 휘돌개차기

돌개차기와 휘돌개차기를 연결하여 난이도를 올릴 수 있다.

1. 돌개차기 후 돌아 디뎌 회전을 한다.

2. 돌아 디딘 후 바로 휘돌개차기를 한다. 이때 디딤발을 디디며 균형을 정확히 잡아주어야 기술의 진행이 안정적이다

3. 기술의 난이도를 올려서 연결할 수 있다. 예를 들어 720° 돌려차기 – 휘돌아 540° 후려차기 또는 뛰어 540° 돌려차기 – 휘돌개차기 등이 있다.

(6) Tornado Kick – Corkscrew kick

You can raise the difficulty level of technique by connecting a tornado to a Corkscrew.

1. After your tornado kick, take a turning step, then spin.

2. After taking a turning step, go straight into your Corkscrew. Your technique can only have stability if you stay properly balanced as you take your turning step.

3. You can increase the difficulty of your technique, then continue connecting it to other techniques. For example, 720° roundhouse kick – box cutter spinning hook kick, or run-up 540 reverse tornado kick– Corkscrew Kick, etc.

▶ 돌개차기 – 휘돌개차기
▶ Tornado Kick – Corkscrew Kick

(7) 옆돌아 540° 후려차기

옆돌기 후 540° 회전하여 후려차기를 한다.

1. 모아 돌개차기가 회전각이 360°라는 기준에서 반바퀴 더 진행하여 찬 발로 착지한다.

3. 착지가 완성되면 공중에서 한번에 540°를 회전하며 후려차기를 한다.

(7) Hyper Hook Kick

After doing a cartwheel, rotate 540° and do a hook kick.

1. A pop tornado kick has a rotation of 360°. Twist an additional half-turn and land on the leg used to kick with.

3. After fully landing, twist 540 ° in the air while doing a hook kick.

▶ 옆돌아 540° 후려차기
▶ Hyper Hook Kick

3. Application techniques of Freestyle Poomsae

(8) 옆돌아 연속 후려차기

옆돌아 540° 후려차기 중간에 바깥차기를 추가한 차기이다.

1. 옆돌기 후 바깥차기를 하고 찬 발로 착지한다.

2. 전 과정이 완성되면, 바깥차기를 찬발로 이어서 후려차기를 한다.

(8) Shuriken Hyper Hook Kick

This is a kicking technique where a twisting kick is added in the middle of a cartwheel-hyper hook kick.

1. Do a cartwheel then a twisting kick, landing on the foot you kicked with.

2. When the previous step is completed, continue into a hook kick with the foot you did your twisting kick with.

▶ 옆돌아 연속 후려차기
▶ Shuriken Hyper Hook Kick

3. 자유품새의 필수기술

(9) 옆돌아 720°

옆돌아 돌개차기에서 차기를 생략하고 720° 회전만 하는 기술이다.

1.옆돌기 후에 기술을 시작하여 720° 회전 후에 착지한다.

2.차기가 없고 회전만 하는 기술로써 시작 시 앞공중과 유사하게 상체를 숙이며 시작한다.

(9) Cartwheel Full Twist Double

This is a technique where the kick is left out in the cartwheel full twist kick, executing only the 720° twisting.

1. After the cartwheel, start your 720° twist, then land upon completing the technique.

2. Since this is a spinning technique without a kick, lower your upper body when you start the technique as you would in a front flip.

▶ 옆돌아 720°
▶ Cartwheel Full Twist Double

3.Application techniques of Freestyle Poomsae

기술 용어 정리 (기술이름 = 시작형태 + 회전각 + 발차기)

분류	트리킹 용어	상용되는 용어	국기원 용어	본 교본 사용 용어
뒤공중	Back Flip*	쭈가리	뒤공중	뒤공중
	X-out	브이 킥	뒤공중 두발 앞차기	뒤공중 두발차기
	Spinning Terada	측전 테라다	뒤공중 앞차기 0단계	뒤공중 이어차기
	T-grab	미르킥	뒤공중 돌아 후려차기	뒤공중 뒤후려차기
	Full Twist*	훌턴 뒤공중	360도	-
	Full Twist Double*	훌턴 더블	뒤공중 720도	-
벨트	Butterfly*	선자	-	모돌기
	B-twist*	벨트	360도 모공중	모돌아 360
	B-twist Kick	벨트킥	360도 모공중 돌려차기	모돌개차기
	B-twist Illusion	일루션	-	모돌아 바깥차기
	B-twist Hyper	벨트 하이퍼	-	모돌아 540 뒤후려차기
	B-twist Double*	벨트 더블	720도 모공중	모돌아 720
하우스턴	Cheat Gainer*	하우스턴	모공중 돌아 후려차기	휘돌기
	Corkscrew*	하우스벨트	540도 모공중	휘돌아 360
	Corkscrew Kick	하우스벨트킥	540도 모공중 돌려차기	휘돌개차기
	Corkscrew Illusion	하우스벨트 일루션	-	휘돌아 바깥차기
	Boxcutter	박스커터	-	휘돌아 540 뒤후려차기
	Corkscrew Double*	하우스벨트 더블	900도 모공중	휘돌아 720
옆돌기	Pop Kick	팝킥	-	모아 돌개차기
	(Cartwheel) Pop Kick	팝턴	-	옆돌아 돌개차기
	(Cartwheel) Hyper Hook	하이퍼훅	-	옆돌아 540 뒤후려차기
	(Cartwheel) Shuriken Hyper Hook	슈리켄 하이퍼훅	-	옆돌아 연속 후려차기
	(Cartwheel) Double Hyper Hook	더블 하이퍼훅	-	옆돌아 900 뒤후려차기
도움닫기	Round off*	측전	측전	측전
	Cartwheel*	옆돌기	-	옆돌기
	Scoot*	스쿳	-	안짚기
	Touch Down Rise*	터치 라이즈	-	바깥짚기

(*) : 발차기가없고회전동작만있는경우

참고문헌

- 대한태권도협회(2020). www.koreataekwondo.co.kr
- 세계태권도연맹(2021). www.worldtaekwondo.org
- 윤수한(2019). 태권도 품새 경기의 올림픽 정식종목 채택과 발전방안. 미간행 박사학위논문, 성균관대학교 일반대학원.
- 임신자, 오철희(2008). 태권도 품새 대회의 심판판정에 대한 인식이 태권도 선수들의 심리상태 및 경기력에 미치는 영향. 한국체육과학회지, 17(4), 403-413.
- 전민우, 임신자, 전익기(2013). 태권도 지도자의 창작품새 경험에 대한 내러티브 탐구. 대한 무도학회지, 15(1), 149-166.
- 전민우(2016). 국가대표 태권도 품새 선수들의 경기력에 영향을 미치는 심리적 방해요인과 대처방안에 관한 연구. 미간행 박사학위논문, 경희대학교 대학원.
- 정병기(2019). 아시아 태권도 수련생들의 품새경기 인식에 따른 ATU 새품새 경기의 발전적 연구. 한국코칭능력개발원, 21(1), 35-42.
- 정재환, 이재환, 김순정(2014). 태권도 품새 경기의 운영요인에 따른 선수와 지도자의 만족도 연구. 한국스포츠 학회지12(4), 115-123
- 차영남, 정재환(2017). 태권도 품새 경기문화의 제고(提高)방안 연구. 한국스포츠학회지, 15(3), 81-89.

References

- Korea Taekwondo Association (2020) www.koreataekwondo.co.kr
- World Taekwondo Federation (2021) www.worldtaekwondo.org
- Yoon Suhan (2019). The adoption of Taekwondo Poomsae as an Olympic Sport and its development. Unpublished doctoral thesis, Sungkyunkwan University General Graduate School.
- Lim ShinJa, & Oh Chul Hui (2008). The effect of Taekwondo athletes' perceptions about referee decisions on their psychological state and competitive ability. Korean Physical Science Association, 17(4), 403-413.
- Jeon Minwoo, Lim, Shinja, & Jeon Eekghee (2013). A narrative exploration of the experiences of Taekwondo coaches and Creative Poomsae. Journal of the Korean Martial Arts Association (15)1, 149-166.
- Jeon Minwoo (2016). A study on the psychological barriers affecting competition and the factors combatting these barriers in national Taekwondo Poomsae Athletes. Unpublished doctoral dissertation, Kyunghee University Graduate School.
- Jeong Byungki (2019). A developmental study of ATU new poomsae competition based on poomsae recognition of Asian Taekwondo Practitioners. Korea Coaching Competency Development Institute, 21(1), 35-42.
- Jung Chaehwan, Kee Jaehwan, Kim Soonjung (2014). A study on the factors affecting athlete and coach satisfaction in relation to the operating factors of Taekwondo Poomsae competition. 12(4), Korea Sport Society. 115-123.
- Cha Yeongnam, Jung, Jaehwan (2017). A study on improving Taekwondo Pomsae Competition Culture. Journal of the Korean Sports Association, 15(3), 81-89.

참고문헌

국기원태권도연구소(2019). 태권도용어사전. 도서출판 다락

References

Kukkiwon(2019). Taekwondo Terminology Dictionary. Darakcompany:Seoul

도움주신 분들

MOOTO, MOOKAS, BM스포츠, 강완진, 홍세진, 이소영, 박기현, 김경규, 차예은, Gloria Cho, Valerie Ho